Bonjour Darling

By

Heather Francis

Note from the Author

This is a true story. I have changed place names relating to our village and the names of dear friends and neighbours in order to protect the identity of those concerned.

To Ronnie, Richard, Katie and Susan
with thanks for their help in launching this work
on an unsuspecting world!

4

Bonjour Darling

Laughter is the best medicine under the sun

Chapter One

Nothing left to lose!

Ouch! I stub my toe yet again on some item of American furnishing, neatly boxed, one of many piled high in every room of my little house in the suburbs of Belfast. I perform some kind of mountaineering feat, just to answer the door. Mingled with this Americana, are all our worldly goods, boxed and awaiting the removal van. By some transatlantic blunder, all the belongings of the American couple, buying our house, have arrived the day before we are about to move out; only the crosses, with which I have laboriously marked each carton, decide whether we arrive in France, with our own furniture, or end up in the middle of the French countryside, living on the set of Frasier!

Nothing can knock my enthusiasm today however, as my husband Ronnie and I, are about to start a new life, in the Charente region of south-west France.

How did we arrive at this moment in our lives? Well, you might indeed ask! Let's just say, it takes one life to end, to contemplate the possibility of starting a new one and end it did. I am forty-eight now, but the beginning of the end started with my fortieth birthday.

Things were just starting to look up for us. I was working part-time in the city, Ronnie had a successful career in banking and our two beautiful children, Richard and Katie, fast becoming independent, were contemplating leaving home for university in Scotland. I remember sitting beside Ronnie, as we drove home from work, through the rich green County Down countryside. The warmth of the evening sun gave me a feeling of security and its sparkle led me to thinking of the exciting adventures we might have, now there would be more time for each other.

What I didn't know was, like many car crashes, metaphorically speaking, we were unaware of what was just around the corner! Over the next weeks, mounting pressure in Ronnie's work saw my husband become withdrawn and very soon the situation would be untenable. He had always been a conscientious worker and his answer was to put in more and more hours, but nothing he did, seemed enough.

Driving into work, on what, unbeknown to us, would be his last day, I noticed his knuckles were white as he grasped the steering wheel and I knew something had to give.

During the next seven years, Ronnie received ill health retirement at age forty and descended into a stress related illness that was as devastating as it was hard to understand. Five of these years, bedridden and unable to bear the light, he remained behind closed curtains. Throughout this time, it was impossible to reach him in his world and doctors had little to offer.

Gradually, spending so much time apart, our relationship became increasingly eroded, until with little left we separated. Spending a year apart, during which time we always kept in touch, I gained confidence, buying my own home and working full-time, while Ronnie, after hitting what can only be described as rock bottom, glimpsed light at the end of the tunnel and started the slow journey back to better health.

I remember the day he rang me in work; he sounded so different, "Heather, I feel I can get better and I want you to be there with me." Slowly, with the help of physiotherapy, Ron gained strength and over the next year, we dated and tentatively rebuilt our trust in each other. Could we get back together, after losing everything we had built up over thirty years of marriage? We needed to wipe the slate clean, leave all the baggage of recent years behind and start again!

By this time our daughter, Katie, had graduated with a degree in French and History of Art from Edinburgh University and was living and working in Paris with the Swiss boyfriend she met during her year out. My son Richard, whose degree was also in French, had a flat of his own here in Belfast and was at the beginning of a promising relationship with Eadaoin, who would later become his wife.

Looking back, since the day I met Ronnie, there had always been a French connection of sorts, in our lives. At that time he was studying French and German at Queen's University, here in Belfast. Further down the line, however, the arrival of children was to change the focus of our lives, as all our energies became channelled into bringing them up.

Our home, however, was always filled with French grammar books, and novels by Sartre and Camus, their presence caught the imagination of our children, shaping their aspirations as they grew to master the art of this foreign language. Now, starting again to rebuild our own lives, the joie de vivre these dusty tomes promised, seemed to point us in the direction of 'La Belle France!'

Ron came to live with me towards the end of that year and together we learned to love and trust each other again. Wanting to put distance between us and the place where things had gone so badly wrong, we gradually began to plan a new life in France, happy to be given a second chance and to share the excitement of the adventure that lay ahead. We had no fear of the future or what we were taking on; when you lose everything, you have nothing left to lose!

Our first thought was where to live in France; it's such a vast country compared to Ireland. We poured over maps and tentatively read everything we could find on regions, climate and geography. Finally, that summer, we set off to explore Provence like many before us, in no small way influenced by the books of Peter Mayle.

I won't go into too much detail of our Provencal trip, just to say we arrived slap bang in the middle of a 'Canicule' or heat wave and naively hired a car with no air-conditioning! Travelling many miles, exploring the area and its beautiful scenery, we wound down our windows in desperation. From outside, the stream of hot air gusting in felt like opening the oven door on the Sunday roast. While inside the car Ron and I were beginning to resemble a couple of oven ready chickens. There was no escape.

The final clue, that perhaps we would be better to consider something slightly further north, came when our estate agent arrived, wearing a bath towel, soaked in ice-cold water and placed on her head like a turban! Driving through the relentless heat, from the back of the car, I watched the rivulets of water trickle down her back, as she went on to explain, the only way she could survive the heat was to soak a nightdress in cold water, and on her return from work, don the aforementioned soggy garment for the rest of the evening.

Back home, maps spread out on the living-room floor again, we started to look further north and paused at La Vendée. Reading about the area, the climate promised warm, sunny summers, less harsh than the extreme heat of the south and property prices in the area were not so expensive, giving us the chance of a bigger house with more outside space.

About this time, we came upon a property company who promised to take the pain out of house-hunting, by setting up houses to view and arranging accommodation for your stay. It seemed the perfect answer, and with their help, we booked our second trip, this time to La Vendée.

Over the next weeks before our departure, I sat at the computer each evening, checking out properties in the area and further south to La Charente. Our budget wasn't large, so I knew wherever we bought, there would be renovation work to do. Refusing to be daunted however, I continued to work my way through endless pictures of dilapidated farm buildings, often amazed at the photos French estate agents were happy to place on their websites. Chuckling at the lines of washing draped across kitchens and in one case a child's potty, left abandoned in the middle of the living room!

It was on one of these late-night forays into cyberspace, that a click of the mouse brought up a photo, which stopped me in my tracks. The 'Old Presbytery' stared out from the computer screen, and almost at once, I was a child again, wide-eyed and transfixed by my father's stories of growing up in an old rectory in the south of Ireland. His descriptions of this beautiful place and his idyllic childhood had been the stuff of my dreams growing up, and here in front of my eyes, was without a doubt, the house of my dreams.

Yes, there it was; old, rather neglected and slightly more French than I remembered - but unmistakably magical. Hurriedly, I read the agent's details; the property was in the centre of a village and the front of the house was accessed by a lane, which swept around behind it, revealing a large park overlooked by the main façade of the property. Double-fronted, it was approached by a grand, if not rather ancient flight of steps. Still owned by the 'commune', having been Church property, it was in very poor repair, the last priest having left the parish several years earlier. What was magical however, was the price - 50,000 euros below our maximum budget!

I called down to Ronnie, unable to curb my enthusiasm, "Come up and see what I've found!" And several minutes later, after extracting himself from the comfort of his armchair, he arrived at my shoulder. Ronnie knew of my family history and the stories of Dad's life growing up in the old rectory. He too had been captivated by my father's reminiscences and recognised at once, the connection with this old, rather tired building and the stuff of my dreams.

"Yes, it's beautiful Heather, but the reason it's so much below our budget is obvious - it needs everything done. It would be a massive project to take on. Besides, we are already booked to go to La Vendée in a week's time. At least there we will be able to experience the properties first hand, rather than just plucking a picture out of thin air.

I knew what Ronnie meant - neither of us was a DIY expert and we had never renovated a property before, but in the quietness of the study, as I looked longingly at the screen, slowly my hand reached for the mouse and pressed PRINT.

Chapter Two

Mission Accomplished

It was the beginning of September, when we arrived at Poitiers airport, and the start of our three-day house-hunting trip to La Vendée. The property company had booked us into a small country hotel, in a little village called Vouvant, which would be central to the properties they had selected for us to view. We would be there for three days, the first two planned out for us and the third free.

The hotel was quaint and typically French, in a cosy, rather 'shabby chic' sort of fashion and as we made our way up to our little attic room, with its floral wallpaper and view of the village church, we shared a feeling of anticipation and eagerness to discover where our new life would begin.

Before we could do anything, however, it was Sunday evening and as the hotel restaurant was closed, we ventured forth to find somewhere to eat. The French countryside stretched out before us in all its vastness and it was several miles before we came upon a restaurant.

Pulling in, we parked by the river, where welcoming lights from inside reflected on the still, calm water. It was quiet and we noticed there were no other cars in the car park, but undeterred and driven by an ever-growing desire for something to eat, we ventured in. Beyond the clean 'gingham-clothed' tables and next to a crackling fire, stood an elderly lady doing her ironing.

Had we accidentally stumbled into someone's front room? Ronnie quickly gathering up his best French, enquired politely if she was open for business. "*Mais oui, monsieur, bien sûr!*" She replied and neatly finishing the garment she was ironing, directed us to a table by the fire. Thus we spent our first night in La Vendée, enjoying delicious rustic French cuisine in Madame's front parlour, where she continued her ironing, only stopping to serve us when her husband announced the arrival of the next course.

The following morning we were awoken at seven by the sound of church bells, while in the village street below, the buzz of French life was already gathering momentum. Lingering over breakfast, we sipped our hot, strong coffee and enjoyed freshly baked croissants and homemade 'confiture'. The brochures for several houses to visit were spread out before us, promising an interesting day's house-hunting ahead.

During the subsequent two days, we went on to view at least six properties. Sadly, however, with each one our initial enthusiasm began to dwindle, as that elusive 'wow factor' so liberally bandied about on property programmes back home, failed to grab us. Was it the region or the houses? We weren't sure, but slightly deflated and confused, we returned to the hotel after an exhausting two-day search and climbing the winding stars to our room, decided to review the situation again in the morning.

Thus, waking on our final day, we found ourselves having seen all the properties chosen for us and still no nearer to finding our new home. As we sat over breakfast, outside the rain fell from a grey and unpromising sky. We looked at each other and Ronnie uttered the words we were both thinking, "This could take forever, Heather! France is so big, where do we go from here?" In a last, desperate attempt, we flicked through the brochures again, methodically rejecting them one by one, until, casting the last one aside, there at the bottom of the pile, was my photocopy of 'The Old Presbytery'.

This time it was Ronnie who pulled the copy out and quietly began to read the details. I sipped my coffee in silence and secretly crossed my fingers under the table. "Do you realise this property is 300 kilometres from here, Heather?" But I knew from the glimmer of hope in his eyes, he had already decided. "You up for it, then?" he chuckled and putting his arm around my shoulder, pulled me towards him. "It will be a long drive, 600 kilometres there and back, but if we find what we came for, then it will be worth it." And so, with the map in front of us, we plotted our route from La Vendée south to La Charente. Our destination would be a little village called Saint-Allier, thirty minutes south of the city of Angoulême.

Through clouds of spray, we hurtled down the motorway towards Bordeaux, keeping pace with the other French drivers, who thought nothing of the road conditions. Every now and then we would disappear completely in the spray of a huge lorry, as we overtook, swept along at the relentless pace of the speeding traffic. Warm inside, we were on a mission and nothing could deter us. After what seemed like an age, we saw a sign up ahead for the small market town of Petit-Villefranche, where the address on my photocopy indicated the estate agent's office was situated in the main street.

The rain had given way to a light drizzle and the sky matched the grey shutters of the lovely old buildings. The little cobbled streets led upwards towards a château, which overlooked the town below; all was quiet, no one wishing to venture forth on this damp September afternoon.

Bumping along the cobbles of the narrow street, our eyes took in the French shop signs: Boulangerie, Tabac, Pharmacie and on the left-hand side towards the end, Immobilier, the agent we were looking for. Pulling in to the kerb, we hopped out and ran towards the window. Like two excited children peering into a sweet shop, our eyes scanned the melange of properties on offer and there in the middle, was the presbytery, exuding its ancient, dilapidated charm and calling out to be loved.

13

From where we stood on the damp pavement, looking past the photos in the window, the shop inside was dark and nothing moved - no sign of life. Was it closed? Could we have come all this way for nothing? Our eyes were drawn to the door and a handwritten note taped to the glass, which indicated, "Back in ten minutes". Our relief was tangible and, in fact, just five minutes passed before the agent returned and holding out a hand, introduced himself as, Laurent.

We were later to discover that Laurent liked to lock up the agency and nip out for a coffee when things got a bit slack. As we would eventually find out, it said a lot about the pace of life in this quiet little French town.

Greetings and explanations over, Laurent was only too happy to take us for a viewing and as he reached into the drawer of his desk, he pulled out a rather large metal key, indicating we should follow him. In the back of his four-wheel drive, we peered out, avidly trying to take in the area, which up to now, we had only fantasised about, and, as we left the town of Petit-Villefranche, Laurent explained Saint-Allier was only five minutes away.

Inside the car it was clear that we would be speaking in French and no sympathy was directed to anyone who fell behind in translation. Ronnie carried on manfully, while I brought up the rear with the occasional "Oui", just hoping I hadn't agreed to anything too binding! Ahead of us, we could see the spire of a church and the outline of the village of Saint-Allier, nestling in a dip between two hills; it beckoned to us through a grey haze.

The road to Angoulême went through the centre of the village and as we entered, passing a large house on the right-hand side, we turned sharply into a lane between it and another house, entitled the 'La Monastère'. A few yards down the lane, turning left and passing behind the gardens of the old monastery and its neighbouring house, we came face to face with two large stone pillars. The huge wrought-iron gates that would have graced this once grand entrance had long gone and a simple wooden gate now barred our way.

14

Already we could see the red-tiled roof with its two metre high chimneys at either end, peering over the stonewall, as Laurent jumped out and opened the gate. Slowly, the car slid through the entrance and we got our first glimpse of the presbytery. In the grey afternoon's dying light, it looked sad and uncared-for, but its unmistakable air of faded grandeur was captivating.

Looking around the huge gardens, to the right of the entrance stood a large barn, which was in remarkably good repair. We later discovered this had been used to house the 'corbière' or horse-drawn hearse, brought out for village funerals. Laurent pointed out two other outbuildings, one a wood store and the other, an old outside toilet that had once served the presbytery.

Peering in, Laurent shone his torch into the dark interior, revealing an old wooden bench with two holes for seats, side by side. Obviously, in the past, it had not been unusual to have company on these visits and looking at each other, we both had to agree, "It must be a French thing?" Finishing our trip around the garden by sampling some grapes from one of the many vines draped around the old barn, we followed Laurent up the steps and into the house.

The old wooden door opened and we piled into the darkness beyond. Trying the light switch with no success, Laurent apologised that the electricity hadn't been switched on and he would have to conduct the tour by torchlight. It didn't really matter though, as by this time Ronnie and I had already fallen in love with the place and no amount of dark decaying rooms he could show us would have put us off!

Never questioning the fact that he made no attempt to open the shutters for added light, we did manage to gather that downstairs contained a living room, dining room, study, kitchen and utility room with downstairs toilet. When I say kitchen, it was just possible to decipher in the torchlight, an old sink in the corner, but this, I assure you, was the only indicator of the room's original function and one would have been forgiven for thinking you had stumbled into a Victorian prison cell!

Up a winding staircase the first floor contained four bedrooms, no family bathroom, but the back bedroom had an adjacent room with a ramshackle shower and toilet. This was just about usable, although definitely not grand enough to deserve the title 'en suite.' Halfway down the long landing, another similar staircase led to a vast loft with huge oak beams.

Everywhere there was clutter, as the commune had been using the presbytery for storage and we delicately picked our way through boxes of ecclesiastical books and religious statues, back down the stairs, to where Laurent showed us a door in the hallway that led down to a series of cellars.

Closely following him, we squeezed along the narrow stone staircase into a labyrinth of rooms, most of which were empty, except for rows of ancient wine racks and some old shelves, which strangely enough, still contained jars of ancient preserves. Finally, entering a room at the front, we discovered the central heating boiler, which amazingly, Laurent announced, was in good working order. The tour over, we stepped out into the garden, not quite sure of what we had just seen, but quite sure that our search was over.

Back at the estate agent's office, Laurent tactfully disappeared into the back, leaving Ronnie and I a few minutes to hastily confer. It was decision-making time. We had travelled hundreds of miles, since our search began and finally, in the little village of Saint-Allier, in the Charente region of the south-west of France, we had found what we were looking for.

Outside, I could just make out the patter of rain again on the shop window, while in the gloomy interior, looking deep into each other's eyes, we both agreed it was a massive project, but the structure of the house was solid and with a bit of elbow grease, it could be liveable, allowing us to remain on site while taking time to get the work done. It would be hard and uncomfortable at first, but what an opportunity to live in such an amazing property. To have a huge garden in which to enjoy long hot French summers, a barn, that at some stage could be converted into holiday gîtes and dare we even dream, to someday have our own swimming pool.

Laurent looked delighted when we told him we would like to go ahead and purchase the property - it was probably one of the easiest sales he had made that year. On our part it was a huge leap of faith, buying a house after only one viewing and that was by torchlight! The adventure, however, was just beginning and after losing so many years of our lives to illness, we grasped it with both hands.

It was agreed with Laurent, that he would send on the 'compromis de vente' or sale agreement, which would arrive with building reports etc, at our house in Ireland. Then it would be up to us to read these and, if satisfied, sign to buy the house. In France, once you have signed the 'compromis', you have a seven-day cooling-off period, during which time you can pull out of the sale, but once this period has expired, you are legally bound to go ahead with the purchase.

Finally, after a firm handshake, we left our estate agent and new friend, Laurent, and began the arduous three-hundred-kilometre drive back to La Vendée and our journey home. Content that at last, it was 'mission accomplished!'

Chapter Three

Stepping into our New Life

The shrill sound of the alarm clock set for 5am, breaks into our night's sleep and through a haze of semi-unconsciousness, the magnitude of this day is beginning to dawn on me. I look around and Ronnie is already in the bathroom. I can hear him throwing water around his face in an effort to persuade himself that this is reality and not some dream. In a few hours time, would he really be boarding a plane destined for Paris and stepping off into a new life?

In the bedroom, our suitcase is packed; this and a small cabin bag contain all we need for the week ahead. We have booked to stay at a gîte in a little village called Agens, a few miles east of Saint-Allier, until we sign the 'acte de vente', to complete the purchase and gain possession of the house. All of which should hopefully coincide with the arrival of our furniture and all our belongings from Ireland.

Excitement is tempered by the hour of the day, as I step out of bed onto the carpet and make my way downstairs, via the carefully boxed Americana. Now that our own boxes have gone, they sit like islands in the gloomy morning light, at last allowing passage to all who sail around them.

Navigating my way into the kitchen, I set out some cereal and milk; there will be no coffee this morning, as even the kettle is on its way to France. In the corner of the kitchen stands a large pet container, inside which slumbers our unsuspecting little Westie, Murphy. Two weeks earlier, we introduced him to this

18

new contraption convincing him it was some kind of luxury bed by placing his blanket inside and encouraging him to look upon it as his new boudoir. Similar to containers in which one would transport cats but at least twice as big, it has a cage door at the front, four wheels on the bottom and is propelled along by a leather strap.

Inside Murphy sleeps oblivious of the luggage label tied to the roof and clearly marked, "Charles de Gaulle Airport", Paris! They say dogs sense everything, but even Murphy hasn't worked out that this safe haven will soon take on the form of a caravan and whisk him off via a Boeing 737, to a new dog's life in the sun!

Ronnie joins us in the kitchen and we give each other a conspiratorial hug, somehow empowering each other with the thought that together we can take on whatever is ahead and determined to make our new life work. The evening before, we said a tearful goodbye to our dear parents and to Richard our lovely son. Leaving them is the downside of this decision, but we know we will be back to Ireland for regular visits and most of all, we look forward to sharing with them our French dream, on the many holidays that lie ahead. Secretly inside, we both really hope that Mum and Dad might consider moving into the gîte in the grounds of the presbytery, but at this early stage that is very much something for the future.

Finally, gathered outside in the early morning light, I pull the door closed, to our little house in Ireland and climb into the taxi. We are bound for the central bus station in Belfast, with tickets to board a coach, for the two-and-a-half hour drive to Dublin airport. Sinking into my seat, I notice the taxi driver is none too happy taking a dog in his cab and I can't help thinking, I look forward to the less judgemental attitude of the French, towards the family pet.

At the station, realising this part of the journey will be long and tiring, we load the cases and the huge crate into the hold of the bus and climbing the steep steps, I carry Murphy down the narrow isle, passed a sea of bemused faces. Eventually, safely landing in our seat, I clutch my loyal pet close to my side and cuddle up to my husband. It is early in the morning and outside, the weather is cold and grey, but inside the bus we feel like the three musketeers, "One for all and all for one!"

Dublin airport is bright and bustling and, pulling Murphy behind us in his trusty crate, we make our way to the information desk to check out the procedure for boarding a dog. It couldn't be a very common occurrence, as we are informed there is no specific check-in desk for dogs, but are instructed to queue at the VIP departure desk across the hall.

Murphy doesn't look particularly impressed to be in the VIP queue, but Ron and I can't help a muffled chuckle, as we take our place in the queue, behind none other than Ronan Keating, from the famous Irish boy band, *Boys Own*.

Smiling at us, Ronan is probably expecting an autograph request, as he realises Ronnie and I have just recognised him, but his attention is quickly diverted to Murphy, who being no respecter of celebrity, is attempting to sniff his leg through the bars of his cage. Having checked in his designer luggage, Ronan takes a quick second glance at Murphy, no doubt wondering if he is going to have to share first class with a hairy mutt!

He needn't have worried however, as the airline's plans for young Murphy were definitely less than luxurious and, as he is wheeled away in his crate, we look at each other, neither of us wishing to imagine the journey that lies ahead for him. Trusting the airline will take good care of our furry friend however, we set off to check our bags in and feeling lighter at last, breathe a sigh of relief as we search out a coffee shop, before boarding our flight to Paris.

Several hours later, at around six in the evening, we find ourselves on the platform of Montparnasse station in central Paris. The tannoy system announces the next train in from Bordeaux, which will arrive at platform two and amongst the bustle of commuters, we stand out with our suitcases and large animal crate.

Many of the passers-by eye us up inquisitively, wondering what kind of creature we are transporting. One or two, unable to resist, take a quick peep inside, declaring, "Ah, Caesar." This I quickly work out, is a reference to the advert for dog food featuring a Westie, which is evidently, also very popular in France. As they raise their arm in a 'Hail Caesar' gesture, we share our first taste of humour, with our new French neighbours.

Looking around, our eyes search through the crowds, for our daughter Katie, who has arranged to meet us, having taken a few days off work to stay at the gîte, until the *act de vente* is signed. Her fluent French will be invaluable to us; also, her French-speaking partner, Olivier, an actor, is filming in nearby Angouleme for the next month and has arranged to meet us at the station there.

Where we stand on the platform, the noise and smells of our new life surround us for the first time and I allow myself to be swept along in the heady Parisian atmosphere. Inside my head, I find my mind speeding like the trains as they roar into the station, already on a journey into the unknown. For the first time in my life I have stepped outside my comfort zone and it feels good!

"Hi Mum". Out of a sea of French announcements, my daughter's voice is raised above the roar of the TGV, as it pulls alongside the platform next to us. Holding each other tightly for a moment, Katie is unable to believe we'll be living in the same country again; she is over the moon to see us and we feel at home instantly, just to be together as a family.

Murphy barks a welcome from inside his crate and at last we can open the door and release him from the container that masqueraded as a safe haven, only to turn into a roller coaster, taking him thirty-thousand feet into the sky and down again! Luckily, he has a short memory and joining us on the platform, is ready to board the train for his next fairground ride.

With great difficulty, the three of us manoeuvre the crate, suitcases and dog, onto the train and after parking the first two in the luggage compartment, proceed along this amazing train, in search of our reserved seats. It would be remiss of me at this point not to mention, how impressive France's fastest train is. Compared to trains I have experienced in Ireland, its seats are plush and spotlessly clean, the design light and modern and it's only when Ron asks Katie how long until departure, that we realise we are already moving through the night, on what feels like a cushion of air.

Falling into our seats, we begin to make ourselves comfortable for the journey to Angouleme. Murphy curls up, half on my lap and half on the seat beside me, our fellow passengers only stopping to effuse, "Oh, Il est très mignon!" So different from the taxi driver in Belfast, who would not have chosen the word sweet, when describing his furry passenger.

Outside, the French countryside speeds by, shrouded in darkness but inside we are in our own little world, chatting animatedly about what we think might lie ahead, reading newspapers and enjoying an impromptu French lesson from Katie, as she tries to improve upon my limited vocabulary.

Time passes and after devouring a hearty supper of fresh, filled baguettes and delicious French coffee, we doze contentedly, until awoken by the tannoy system announcing our imminent arrival, at Angouleme station. With only a short window of time before the train continues on to Bordeaux, we leap into action and like a military operation, when the train stops file out onto the platform. A platform that unbeknown to us now, is to become the stage, for so many emotional reunions in the years to come.

From the inside of the station, Olivier emerges through the disembarking crowd and hugs Katie. What luck that he just happens to be filming here; it means he can spend time with Katie and also help us settle in. Tonight his job is to take us to the car hire pick-up point, help us to load up, after which, we are to drop him off at his hotel in the *centre ville*, before heading via

Saint-Allier, to the village of Agens and the comfort of our awaiting gîte.

As Ron gets used to the gears of the hire car, we make our way through the steep streets of Angouleme and are reminded that this is an old fortified city, built on a high promontory and surrounded by city walls. In the summer it is famous for its classic car racing through the streets and rumour has it, that the atmosphere reminds one of Monte Carlo - a bit hard to imagine tonight, however, as it is bitterly cold and pouring with rain.

In the dark there is a complicated one-way system and we are glad of Olivier's directions, as we navigate our way through the narrow cobbled streets, finally arriving at the main square, to park in front of the brightly lit hotel. Congratulating each other on having made it this far, we wave Olivier off to the comfort of his hotel room and switching the wipers to double speed, point the car in the direction of Saint-Allier, on the last leg of our journey.

Half-an-hour's drive from Angoulême, through a rainy windscreen, we can just make out a church spire and realise the village of Saint-Allier is coming up ahead. Frantically wiping the steam from the car windscreen, we sit bolt upright in our seats like a group of meerkats, peering through the gloom, desperate to see our new home, we make our way along the sleepy main street, as Ron, slowing down, pulls in opposite the boulangerie.

There she is, innocently slumbering in the lamplight, shutters closed against the relentless drizzling rain, unaware that help is at hand and the years of neglect are almost over. For us it's been a long day and promising to return, we start the engine in the silent street and looking back over our shoulders, until our new home is out of sight, head off to our gîte and the thought of a good night's sleep.

At the end of a dark lane the family dog, barking loudly, announces our arrival as we pull into the farmyard. Through the darkness, a light from one of the windows indicates the occupants are still up and I breathe a sigh of relief. Susan and

James, an English couple, who moved to the region a few years earlier, own the gîte. They have worked incredibly hard and with the aid of local French artisans, have managed to create two holiday homes and are about to embark on a third. It is by now almost eleven at night and through the gloom, Susan emerges from the warmth of the farmhouse kitchen to greet us, closely followed by Jo, their pet Jack Russell.

She is wearing a pair of heavy wellington boots, several jumpers and a scarf. Under the night sky, her face still flushed from sitting by the wood-burning stove, she looks happy and relaxed, greeting us warmly with the traditional three kisses. Due to the lateness of the hour, we enjoy a brief, but informative tour of the property and perhaps, recognising in each other a kindred spirit, agree to meet up again over the next few days to share our stories.

Happy that our hosts have created a home from home, we say goodnight, allowing Susan to disappear back to the warmth of the farmhouse. Closing the door behind her, I look round the rustic kitchen with its welcoming ambience and feel for the first time that we are actually going to live in France. Eventually climbing into bed, with Murphy snugly curled up in his basket, we whisper "*Bonne nuit!*" before the three of us fall into a deep and dreamless sleep.

Several days pass and the morning of the '*acte de vente*' dawns dry but still very overcast. Wrapping my dressing gown tightly around me, I head into Katie's room to wake her for the big day, only to be greeted by a very hot-looking face, peering over the edge of the duvet. "I am so sorry, mum, but I feel awful and I don't think I'll be able to make it to the notaire's office." It is obvious Katie has a temperature and is coming down with a bout of the flu.

Very quickly, I realise she is going to miss this special occasion, for which she has travelled so far and, of course, we are going to miss our fluent French speaker, at a time when we need all the help we can get with this important legal procedure. Motherly instincts don't take long to kick in, however, and after making her comfortable, I go downstairs to prepare a warm drink and some paracetamol. The gîte kitchen is clean and cosy and Murphy wags his tail in welcome, but already adopting the laid-back French attitude, remains in his basket, as I prepare breakfast.

Everybody fed and the patient medicated, we dress and get ready for the day, kindly, Susan has volunteered to pop in and check on the patient while we are out. The arrangement is to meet the estate agent at the presbytery at two o'clock. It is part of French purchasing law, that the buyer should be shown the property one final time, before signing the '*acte de vente*.' Presumably this is to ensure that they are entirely aware of what they are purchasing, in order to avoid any comeback afterwards, when an unfortunate buyer may unwittingly discover he or she has purchased a pig in a poke.

After a final look around the property, we will then proceed to the notaire's office, where we will meet up with the notaire himself and the Mayor of Saint-Allier, who is to act as the vendor for the sale of the property.

The sun is making a valiant attempt to peer through a watery sky, as Ron and I drive in through the two grand pillars and pull up in front of the presbytery. Laurent, our estate agent and his colleague Anna, an attractive Dutch girl with really good English, are waiting to greet us at the bottom of the steps. In a flurry of "bonjours" and the usual three kisses apiece, they share our excitement, as we pile up the steps and into the presbytery for our official tour of inspection.

At the top of the steps I stop and turning round, take in the view of the garden and the hills beyond. Is this really what will greet me each morning when I open my door? Little do I know yet, how special this vantage point will become to me. Over the next years I am to find myself sitting here, watching the changing seasons and sharing my summer days with the little lizards that scurry around the steps in the hot summer sun.

Back to reality I catch up with the others, as Laurent gives us a tour of the house. There is still rubbish everywhere and Anna apologises and promises she will get some men from the commune to clear everything before we move in. Pausing in what would have been the priest's bedroom, Laurent laughs and pulls something from amongst the clutter, handing it to Ronnie. "There you are - something to remind you, of the history of your house!"

We find ourselves looking at a very old, intricately carved crucifix, which must have adorned the walls of the presbytery for many years. It is hard not to notice the extremely pained expression on the face of Christ however and we both feel a bit unsure exactly where it will fit into our decor, without traumatising any future visitors!

Having looked in each room, including the cellars, and declaring ourselves happy (happy that is to take on a massive renovation project!), we sign the appropriate declaration and head for the notaire's office in the neighbouring village of Montbusson.

Inside the notaire's office is rather dark, perhaps due to the inclement weather outside but there is that unmistakable smell of musty paper and bureaucracy. Our group of four is ushered into the notaire's office by his secretary and greeted by himself and the Mayor. Kisses are obviously not the order of the day on this rather auspicious occasion and so it's formal handshakes all around.

The mayor turns out to be a rather handsome man in his late forties and smiles pleasantly as we greet him with his full title Monsieur Le Maire. He in turn introduces the notaire, a tall well-built man in his late fifties, who, with a commanding air of authority, peers over a pair of horn-rimmed glasses, curious no doubt, to meet, yet another foreign couple hoping to find happiness in his tiny community.

Chairs are carefully arranged in a line in front of his desk and we are each allocated a seat. Ronnie and I are placed directly in front of the notaire and furnished with a ballpoint pen each.

There is a lot of French being spoken and I am hoping inside, Ronnie is keeping pace with the proceedings.

Everything is conducted in a friendly manner however, and the notaire begins by asking Ronnie and me, how we come to be buying in France. Between the two of us, we share a convoluted version of our story and everyone is eager to wish us much happiness in our new venture and to assure us that we have chosen a very friendly and welcoming part of France, in which to set up home.

Niceties over, it is down to business and the positioning of our seating arrangements becomes apparent, as a conveyor-belt system of form filling begins! Everything appears to have to be signed in triplicate and with great efficiency forms are passed to Ronnie, who signs and passes them to me to sign and return to the notaire. This well-oiled system continues for what seems like a very long time, until finally grinding to a halt, the notaire leans back in his chair and reaching out his hand, declares, "Congratulations Madame et Monsieur Kennedy, you are now the proud owners of, The Old Presbytery at Saint-Allier."

Formalities over, we take our leave and finding ourselves outside in the car park, kisses are now the order of the day, as we share our excitement with Laurent and Anna - we, as the new owners of our first French home, and Anna and Laurent, as the recipients of ten percent of the purchase price. Discreetly Laurent reaches into his car and presents Ronnie with a bottle of Champagne, wishing us, "Santé," to the start of our new life in France.

Chapter Four

Moving-in Day

The sixth of December, moving-in day, dawns grey and damp. Due to bad weather in the English Channel, our furniture has been delayed for a week and Katie, unable to be here for the big day, has had to return to Paris for work. Luckily Susan and James are able to extend the gite rental for an extra week, while we await the arrival of all our worldly goods. During this time, we manage to share many a lovely meal around their wood-burning stove in the kitchen and as it turns out, our time far from being wasted, becomes a valuable period of learning, about renovation and local artisans, not to mention the chance to cement a great new friendship.

It's hard to describe how I am feeling right now, as we wait in the empty house for the arrival of the removal company. Everything looks larger than life: the ceilings are really high and the rooms grand and imposing, yet in contrast, everything is covered in years of dirt and grime, the electrics look antiquated and decidedly dodgy; ancient floral French wallpaper falls from the walls and in the kitchen, the old porcelain sink hangs precariously in a dark corner, desperately trying to reassure us, "Yes, this is the kitchen!"

Strangely though, at no time do I feel worried or afraid and deep down inside, there is a wonderful sense of contentment, this is where I am meant to be and, for the first time in many years, everything feels vibrant and alive.

Walking around the house, I reassure Ron that everything will come together, as we dare to put our heads around each door in turn. In the back bedroom, where the old showerhead lies in the ancient, dirty and cracked basin, the walls of the adjoining bedroom are badly marked around the chimneybreast and the old marble fireplace. This, we have been told, is a testimony to damage suffered in the great storm of 1999. The estate agent has furnished us with proof of repairs completed to the huge chimney at that time, when it almost had to be rebuilt, but there is now still much refurbishment required to return the walls to their former glory.

Each room has its own problems, the best of which would be the living and dining rooms, where apart from decoration and rewiring, there is the least to be done. Surprisingly, as we discovered earlier, the house has partial oil-fired central heating and there is a radiator in both these rooms, two of just five radiators in the property, the others being in the kitchen, one of the bedrooms and the hallway. We were told the commune had saved up to install it about ten years earlier, as the priest was getting older and found winters in the big house more and more difficult. The huge boiler located in the cellar, thankfully, continues manfully to turn out the heat, when called upon.

It is obvious from what we have heard, that churches all over France are becoming less and less supported and that parishes are being closed and presbyteries sold as money becomes more of an issue. Indeed, the beautiful little church here in Saint-Allier is only used for weddings and funerals now.

At this point we are oblivious to the fact that the church may no longer play a big part in village life, but its huge bell is very much at the centre of things and its ringing will soon set the rhythm for our lives, as it does for all the villagers.

It's not the church bell, however, that catches our attention and calls us away from our tour of works, but a very familiar sound, ringing out over the normal buzz of French village life, streaming through the open windows and coming from the boulangerie on the other side of the main street. The unmistakable Northern Ireland accent can be heard clearly, demanding directions of the confused shopkeeper, who no doubt, can understand nothing. Ron and I can't resist a smile to each other, before gathering our wits together, we make for the front door and across the street to the shop.

Entering the boulangerie, we greet Madame and the other bemused shoppers with the customary, "Bonjour, messieurs-dames" and, wasting no time, hastily introduce ourselves to the two burly removal men. Speaking no French, they would appear to be under the impression, that if they repeat their demands loudly enough, the language barrier will magically fall down, a bit like the walls of Jericho! Evidently their relief is tangible, as they encounter the sound of a familiar accent and as I point to the house across the street, they are quick to return to the safety of their huge lorry.

When they finally manage to manoeuvre the enormous vehicle into place in front of the house, there is just enough room for the traffic to pass and a queue of impatient French drivers is finally released to continue their journey, with only a couple of tooting horns and one cry of 'merde!'

As box after box of belongings pile up in the appropriate rooms, I find myself in the kitchen, tearing open cartons marked kitchen equipment, in a desperate attempt to locate the kettle and teapot. These men, as they remind me, have travelled hundreds of miles and haven't had a decent cup of tea since they drove off the ferry at Calais. Enough to send any Irish workman into a state of withdrawal!

When the kettle finally does emerge from its packing case, I am prepared, having bought the appropriate tea bags, milk and sugar. Breathing a sigh of relief, while filling the said appliance, I set about searching out the nearest socket. Plugging it in, I arrange the mugs on the edge of the old sink, add milk and sugar as instructed and begin to relax. Everything is falling in to place - in no time, we will be clasping mugs of hot tea and declaring ourselves, "home at last."

Lapsing into that comfortable feeling one gets in a place, when sustenance is about to arrive, I reach up optimistically to unplug the kettle and disaster strikes! Alas, the plug doesn't come out of the socket; the socket comes out of the wall, closely followed by an array of bare wires and a cloud of dust. This time, it's my turn to cry out the English equivalent of the popular French expletive, as I look in horror at the socket hanging loosely from the wall, still attached to the plug and kettle.

From upstairs, Ronnie bursts into the kitchen, not knowing quite what to expect, but just hoping everybody is still alive and well. Quickly weighing up the situation, he enquires if I am all right, to which I feebly reply, "It just came off in my hand!" Retrieving the kettle, he carefully unplugs it from the hanging socket and passing it to me, with a cheeky smile, demands, "Just one sugar dear!" Rather than cry, we simply look at each other and laugh, while standing around in our so-called kitchen; Ronnie, the two burly removal men, and myself, clutch our cups of hot tea, realising alas, we are indeed 'home at last!'

The rest of the day is spent laboriously trying to find things from the endless boxes, cleaning what we can to make the place as habitable as possible and eventually erecting our bed, beneath the ugly, stained walls in the back bedroom. Resting serenely in the middle of all the mess and peeling walls, it stands a testament to my dream - of how the house will look when finished. Arrayed in the beautiful French toile duvet cover and pillowcases, I purchased in Belfast, it exudes an air of sanity, in the surrounding madness.

Finally, we collect Murphy from Susan and James, who had kindly let him remain in the gîte, while we moved in. He scurries up the steps and in through the front door to be met by a profusion of new smells, intermingled with the familiar scents of things from home.

Eventually discovering his bed in the so-called kitchen, he no doubt thinks to himself, "Is this it?" Several roller-coaster rides and hundreds of miles travelled, to find one's new bedroom is no better than a Victorian prison cell! I don't think he is entirely impressed, but at least we are together and being part of the pack is what matters most to Murphy.

By eleven o'clock in the evening, we are absolutely exhausted and mounting the stairs to bed, set about our ablutions in a very makeshift bathroom. Back in the bedroom the luxury toile bed calls invitingly and as we climb in, pulling the duvet around us, the sight we see, when daring to peep over the top, is one of complete chaos, while underneath, turning off the light, our dreams are of 'La vie Française' and our beautiful new home in France.

Several days having passed, each piece of furniture has gravitated to its final resting place and clearly defined areas have begun to emerge. We now have a room to sit in, where one can escape the mess and enjoy a cup of coffee. Speaking of hot beverages brings me back to the earlier debacle...with the socket in the kitchen.

To my surprise, last night, around six o'clock, we were disturbed by sounds coming from outside and peering from the landing window to the street below, anxiously watched, as a car and trailer stopped in front of the house. Three burly French men in dungarees jumped out. Sounding animated and jovial, they set about placing a ladder up against the front wall of the presbytery and, in the darkness of the landing, Ronnie and I looked on in confusion and slight trepidation, at this uninvited invasion of our home.

Much running back and forward ensued, between our house and the house diagonally across from us, where by now, another ladder had been carefully erected. To our right, as we watched, one of the men was at the top of his ladder, with what looked like a long line of bulbs hanging from his shoulder and trailing down to the pavement below. His accomplice, taking the other end, proceeded to climb his ladder and on the given instruction of "Allez" the bulbs were lifted and stretched across the road, well out of the reach of any passing traffic.

In front of our eyes, from our secret vantage point, we watched as, accompanied by a loud cheer, the coloured lights sprang into life. Ron and I looked out into the night from our little spot on the landing and like two children watching for Santa Claus, realised Christmas had arrived in Saint-Allier!

It was the doorbell that finally drew our eyes away from the hypnotic colours of the festive lights, as we suddenly realised that one of the men was at the front door. My first thought was, oh dear - a barrage of French is about to be launched my way! I knew Ronnie even found it difficult, with the local accent and the speed at which these enthusiastic discourses were conducted, but we were in France now, so girding our loins and putting on a brave smile, we threw open the door and greeted our unexpected visitor with an enthusiastic if not slightly quizzical, "Bonsoir, monsieur?"

In the darkness, the shape of a tall, slim man in his mid-forties is silhouetted against the lamplight, his hand outstretched, he introduces himself as, Monsieur Noël, a member of Saint-Allier commune and the local village electrician. It is at this point a conversation with our next-door neighbour, the Mayor, springs to mind, when he had recommended monsieur Noël to do our rewiring, saying he would also mention our predicament with the kitchen socket to him, when they next met.

It all started to make sense and with great delight, we invited him in. I have to say at this point, the irony of our new visitor's name did not go unnoticed, literally translating as Mr Christmas! Indeed, if it had been Father Christmas himself, Ronnie and I could not have been more delighted, as we led him in to the kitchen, to view the offending socket.

Monsieur Noël turned out to be a very pleasant man, with a business-like approach which inspired confidence and it was agreed that he would return again the next day, to make safe the socket, at which point he would set about preparing an estimate to rewire the whole house. We discussed with him that we wanted the wiring sunk into the walls and re-plastered, rather than, as is so often found in French houses, channelled down the outside of the walls and he agreed to take this into account in his '*devis*'.

At last, things were starting to happen and we couldn't be happier to employ our first local Frenchman; he in turn told us how happy the villagers were, that their old Presbytery was to be rescued.

The village of Saint-Allier, like so many rural French towns, has lost a lot of its young people to the big cities and the locals, favouring the *pavillon*, or modern French bungalow, have vacated much of the older housing stock. The refurbishment of the presbytery will mean new life at the heart of the village and the salvation of one of its most significant buildings.

As monsieur Noël prepared to leave, he explained that it was tradition to hang the Christmas lights from the presbytery and he hoped we didn't mind. Ronnie, who by now, was gaining confidence in his ability to communicate, thought he might go for a bit of humour and jokingly suggested, "It was no problem, just as long as they weren't running them off our electricity!"

A pause ensued, as we both waited for the inevitable smile to cross monsieur Noël's handsome face, but alas, I think the comedy aspect, must have been lost somewhere in translation. Rather than join us in a friendly chuckle, he actually thought Ronnie was being serious and went on to spend at least five minutes insisting that the commune was not intending to steal our electricity, but had an independent source of power for its decorations. It was too late to explain our attempt at humour however, and reassuring him that we were quite happy with the situation, he wished us, 'Joyeux Noël' and disappeared into the night.

The next day is spent going around the house with monsieur Noël, marking the walls with large crosses, where we would like the sockets to be situated. It is quite an onerous task, as once they are fitted they won't be able to be changed and so we try to think carefully how they will be used, only slowing down slightly, as we realise the price is rising steeply with each socket.

Later that evening in the so-called kitchen, as I rustle up something in the microwave, the phone rings in the hallway and I am greeted by the enthusiastic tones of Katie, ringing from Paris. "Hi Mum, I've been thinking." I must just stop here, as it is important to point out, that when Katie has been thinking, one can never be quite sure what is coming next. And today was to be no exception.

"I just felt what a shame it would be for you and Dad to be all alone in France for your first New Year's Eve and, as you haven't really got to know anyone yet, my friends and I are going to come down and help you bring in the new year, French style! There will only be six of us and don't worry Mum, we are going to do all the cooking and you and Dad can put your feet up."

Gathering my wits I hastily reply, "Wait a minute, Katie, this place still looks like a derelict bomb site and we haven't got to Ikea yet, to get the kitchen," but before I can go any further, she jumps in, " It will be ok, Mum, we'll manage, anyway I've already asked them and they don't mind roughing it. It will be our treat and a great start to your first year in France."

Sensing a fait accompli, I reluctantly think to myself, well, we definitely wouldn't be lonely and it might even be fun to have the house filled with young French people, rather than just Ron and I rattling around on our own. As I come off the phone however, I think to myself, I will have to break this one to Ron gently!

It takes several days of gentle persuasion, to finally convince Ron, that having a house load of French twenty-somethings for New Year, is a good idea and indeed as far as I am concerned, the jury is still out on that one.

If it has done anything, however, it has spurred us on to set about creating the kitchen and with that in mind, I have been frantically measuring the walls and searching my Ikea catalogue for suitable units. The kitchen is basically square in shape, with a window looking out over the park at the back of the house. The view of the garden from this window is quite beautiful, as the house being built over cellars, means the windows on the first floor are quite high up.

Although not enormous in size, there is ample room for free-standing units around the walls and a table by the window. On the back wall there is a useful pantry and a door leading into a downstairs toilet, this room is big enough to be a utility area and will also house the washing machine, tumble dryer and freezer.

Over the next days, we make the kitchen our priority and, after washing down the woodwork and painting the walls a pale buttery yellow, it starts to take on a fresh, clean look and even the old sink seems happier, sporting a very attractive blue gingham skirt, to cover the pipes and to provide a hiding place for the gas cylinder, that hopefully one day soon, will be connected to a cooker.

Luckily, at the weekend, Katie and Olivier arrive down for a couple of days and prove very useful, especially Olivier's knowledge of French shops. With his help, we discover an enormous electrical store called Darty, and spend a very exciting afternoon choosing appliances.

It's amazing when you haven't had a cooker, washing machine or tumble dryer for a while, just how exciting this can be. Olivier, with his passion for cooking, points me towards a beautiful range cooker and explains passionately, as only a Frenchman can, the amazing delicacies one could produce on such an appliance. I think he is probably looking forward to having a go himself, when they come down for New Year, as he seems particularly keen that we choose an amazing 'Rolls Royce' of a cooker!

After an hour or two, having finally selected the basic essentials to get our kitchen up and running, we agree a delivery date of the middle of next week with the attractive young assistant and, heading off to find a restaurant for our evening meal, unanimously agree, no one wishes to endure another offering from the microwave!

Chapter Five

A Record-breaking Feat!

With Christmas just ten days away, Ron and I meticulously plan the last stage of 'Operation Kitchen', which basically involves a mad dash to Bordeaux, where our nearest Ikea outlet promises the flat-pack answer, to La cuisine of our dreams.

It's around one o'clock by the time we hit the road, on what turns out to be a crisp, bright winter's day. Inside the little rented Renault Clio, our main mode of transport, until the arrival of a new Peugeot in January, Murphy looks out the back window, his tail wagging in misguided anticipation of perhaps, some leafy walk to come. As usual in a bout of misplaced sentimentality, I have persuaded Ron, Murphy would be better with us, something I may well live to regret later!

Clutching my strategically marked Ikea catalogue, we set off for the motorway to Bordeaux, passing through a series of sleepy little French towns, (to all seemingly intensive purposes) deserted, until everything reopens again at three in the afternoon. The only signs of life for now come from the occasional little café, where inside, the important business of lunch is well underway.

After a minor map-reading mishap and a bout of confusion involving the one-way system, passing through the small town of Coutras, we finally find ourselves on the slip road of the main motorway to Bordeaux. Edging along tentatively, we await patiently, our chance to join the traffic. There is something in the tension of the moment, reminds me of an athlete receiving the baton in a relay race and as soon as a space presents itself, we grab it and are off.

There follows a relatively peaceful hour and a half, as we are carried along in a sea of cars, until the first signs for *Bordeaux Centre* start to appear and tension inside the little Renault Clio begins to rise, as we desperately try to read each one. Just up ahead, sparkling in the bright, winter sunlight, the bridge over the river Gironde reaches into the sky, a testament to modern engineering, as it stretches across the river, taking the colourful ribbon of traffic safely to the other side and setting us down on the periphery of Bordeaux city.

With Ron's excellent sense of direction and a bit more frantic sign reading, we soon find ourselves entering the car park of the enormous Ikea and parking not far from the entrance, I hop out, releasing Murphy from the boot to stretch his legs. Despite a disappointing landscape, devoid of any kind of vegetation, he manages to find a convenient tree and after a quick comfort break, is returned to the car to enjoy a doggy chew, while Ron and I, feeling more relaxed, head for the entrance.

I must point out here, that as with every shopping trip Ronnie and I make, our first port of call, will always have to be the coffee shop. Just between you and me, I find this rather frustrating, as my idea would be to do the shopping first and enjoy a coffee after, as a kind of reward. Experience has taught me, however, a happy husband, makes for a much more agreeable day out and so we find ourselves joining the masses over a hot drink and something unpronounceable from the Swedish pastry section.

Finally, Ron feels he has had enough coffee to prop himself up for the ordeal ahead and we set off following the floor arrows like Dorothy on the yellow-brick road. I did mention when we arrived, we were feeling relaxed, well this state of affairs continues and, as we pass through each department, taking in the must-have household items, we do not notice the time pass, or the weight of the enormous yellow sack, which is rapidly filling.

I think neither of us dreamt just how good it would feel to be out amongst civilisation again, as opposed to being trapped in the middle of a dusty renovation project. Therefore, mesmerised by the passing objects, we turn into contestants on The Generation Game, our yellow sack containing everything but a cuddly toy!

Eventually reality brings us back to earth with a bump, as we realise we are in the centre of the kitchen department and the importance of our mission strikes us once again. Guiding Ronnie towards the free-standing units we have selected from the catalogue, we both agree they are perfect. Our selection comprises a long beech-topped unit with drawers beneath, which will provide a good work surface and storage, a matching dishwasher cabinet, also topped with a solid-beech work surface and a smaller unit with two attractive wicker baskets.

To help out with storage, we select some shelves for the wall, with a stainless steel rail below, to hang pots and utensils. In my mind's eye, our lovely kitchen is taking shape and with the handsome range cooker at the heart of it, I begin to dream of cooking my first proper meal. Finally, breathing a sigh of relief we head towards the desk, to put in our order and arrange delivery.

It's not long before we find ourselves at the head of the queue, where an efficient assistant is perched at an impressive looking computer. Nothing is too much trouble as she keys in the items on our list, helpfully throwing in a smattering of English to put us at our ease and insure the order is correct. Jovially we share with her, our relief at the prospect of a new kitchen, especially with the festive season almost upon us, and a crowd of guests about to descend for New Year.

With the mention of the word Christmas, alas, her face drops, "*Mais Monsieur, desolé…*" Now in my limited experience of the French language, the word *desolé* never did bode well and on this occasion, it lived up to its reputation. Janine, our helpful assistant looks crestfallen, as she explains that there will be no deliveries in our region, until the new year.

Well, if Janine looks crestfallen, Ronnie and I look positively devastated; perhaps a little naively, the thought had never crossed our minds, that delivery may not be possible before Christmas and taking in the enormity of what she is saying, we face again the idea of Christmas with no kitchen. Janine however, not wishing to lose a sale, suggests the other obvious solution, "You could take it today of course, if you have a big enough car; it does come flat-packed."

In my mind I have a picture of the little Renault Clio outside in the car park, with a sleeping dog curled up in the boot; is it possible to get a whole kitchen into a Renault Clio? I have heard of competitions to get as many people as possible into a Mini; some attempts being quite successful, but people are so much more pliable than kitchen units!

We look at each other and with no other option available to us, agree, "Let's ring the Guinness Book of Records, we're going to give it a go!" And so we take the print-out of our order, pay Janine and head for the pick -up bay.

Outside, darkness has fallen and being almost six in the evening, the only noise that can be heard, is that of the rush-hour traffic leaving Bordeaux for the suburbs. In the bright lights of the pick-up bay, our little Clio is dwarfed by the vastness of the place and for some reason every car in the vicinity looks like a four-wheel drive.

Out of the shadows, a couple of muscular young Frenchmen appear, pushing our kitchen on two overloaded trolleys. They glance at us, then at the little Clio and then back to us again; no French is necessary, their expressions are universally understood. Ron and I try to cover our embarrassment with an over-enthusiastic air of confidence, "*C'est pas de problème*!" But as we open the boot and a rather dazzled young Murphy staggers into the bright, fluorescent light, it is obvious they have us summed up - another couple of mad foreigners.

41

The game begins in earnest, as the back seats are laid flat and bits of kitchen go in, only to be taken out again and tried at yet another angle. Eventually, realising the male of the species to be more competitive in these matters, I happily leave the men to solve the puzzle and decide to take Murphy for a walk around the concrete car park.

Ambling about in the darkness, Murphy eventually manages to find yet another tree in what is basically a wilderness, although after giving it a cursory sniff he wanders off again, deciding that no other dogs have passed this way - probably because their owners had more sense than to bring them to such a desolate place.

Finally, we get the call to return to the car, where the pavement is now clear of any stray kitchen parts and Ron is standing triumphantly over his record-breaking feat. With a rather smug, yet slightly nervous grin, he suggests we hop in and hit the road. Strangely enough, as you might have guessed, this is easier said than done and as I open the rear door, the front passenger seat being laid flat and buried under long work surfaces, I point out that there is nowhere to sit. The interior of the car is literally stacked to the roof with boxes.

"Of course there is, dear, just under here, if you balance on the edge of the rear seat and keep your head down under this beech work surface, you should just fit in. The dog can go at your feet."

And so we set off, with me bent double under a beech work surface, with my nose two inches from Murphy's and Ron trying to drive, with no visibility through the rear screen mirror and a large plank of wood, balancing precariously by the side of his head.

I cannot describe the journey that ensues, but if I tell you that it takes us an hour just to get through the rush-hour traffic and cross the bridge, before we even embark on the two-hour motor-way drive back to Saint-Allier. Ron is panicking the whole time, in case we are spotted by the French Police and I am just wondering, if I will ever be able to straighten up again!

It is almost eight o'clock when we pull up at the foot of the presbytery steps, unable to believe we have made it home, with the kitchen and ourselves, still miraculously intact. Gradually acclimatising to the upright position again, we congratulate each other, on the final success of 'Operation kitchen'. That is until we realise, we are standing at the bottom of a very large flight of steps.

The next half hour sees 'Operation Kitchen' recommence, as we haul and pull the flat-pack units up the steps and into the house. Above us the evening sky is filled with myriad stars, and we stop to take a deep breath. Our new life may be full of challenges, but while the only sound in the night air, is the sound of our breathing and the distant hoot of an owl, we realise once again, it is about being alive and building a new life!

Chapter Six

Candlelight and Peeling Wallpaper

The morning of the 24th of December dawns crisp and seasonal. In the presbytery there are virtually no clues as to the imminent festive celebrations. Ron and I have just emerged from a two-day episode of the Krypton Factor, where the task was to construct a kitchen out of a pile of wood, thousands of nuts and bolts, an Allen key and a list of instructions a mile long. Let's just say we are still married... just! And there is now a fully functioning kitchen in place, minus the dishwasher, which is to be delivered in the new year.

When I say we have no decorations in place, that is not quite true, as we do have a large red foil sausage hanging from the front door. The said item was attached under the cover of darkness, by someone from the commune and would appear to be masquerading as a Christmas cracker. Each house in the village has been gifted with a similar sausage or cracker, in varying colours. Apart from these decorations, there are however, a few rather strange additions to the festive scene, which have appeared in our village and many of the nearby towns.

They take the form of rather life-like figures, found scaling the exterior walls of some of the houses. Carrying a sack over one shoulder they hang precariously from a drainpipe. Now, if the same characters had been perched on a chimney, I would have immediately thought, Santa Claus, but these characters bear more resemblance to a cat burglar. I first noticed them when coming home in the dark one evening and my immediate thought was to ring the police. It still gives me a little shiver, when I head off to bed at night, thinking there might be a *Père Noel* scaling my exterior wall!

We are leaving the village behind this morning however, as we head towards Petit-Villefranche to collect the Christmas turkey. In front of us the chateau hangs in a shroud of mist, as if floating in a cloud like some fairytale castle, above the busy little town. We park in the square, where a fountain stands in the centre; its water either frozen or reserved for the hot sunny days of summer.

Everywhere people hurry about their business, carrying boxes containing chocolate logs from the patisserie, foie gras and cheeses from the delicatessen, oysters and other such delights. Their faces are as yet unfamiliar to us, as we head towards the butchers, where monsieur Bernard, the master butcher, has promised to reserve us one of his best free-range turkeys.

After a twenty-minute wait in the queue, during which time I struggle to eavesdrop on the French conversations going on around me, I find once again, that every one talks so fast, I can understand very little. Finally, as monsieur Bernard hands over a large white plastic bag containing our turkey, I manage a confident sounding, "*Merci Monsieur et bonnes fêtes*" and heading back out to the street, vow to dig out my French study tapes as soon as the festivities are over.

Our shopping trip culminates with a visit to the Boulangerie for some fresh bread. Here, behind the counter, an array of amazing creations, depicting the many aspects of Christmas, are fashioned in sponge cake, icing and cream for our delectation. Ron and I, '*comme d'habitude*,' give in to temptation, deciding on a tasty looking chocolate log and watch in admiration, as the assistant places it in a cake box and ties it delicately with coloured ribbon. Looking up with a smile, she enquires politely, *"C'est pour offrir, madame?"* *"Non,"* I reply, *"C'est pour moi!"*

On our return to the presbytery, pulling in through the old stone pillars, we draw up at the foot of the steps and glancing momentarily in the rear-view mirror, I catch a glimpse of a slim-looking gentleman, casually dressed in corduroy trousers and a light-coloured jacket, making his way up the drive towards the car. As he approaches, I notice he would be in his early-to-mid sixties, of light build, with a smart, almost military-like upright stature and a head of steely, grey hair brushed to one side in a debonair quiff. The overall picture bearing a striking resemblance to an old American movie star.

To date we haven't really met many of the villagers and are quite surprised to see one of them daring enough to venture in and say hello. Most people seem curious, but are more than a little scared to confront the language barrier. Climbing out of the car, on what is a chilly, grey morning, Ron and I head over to greet our intrepid visitor and are met with a lovely gentleman, who rather shyly says, "Hello," in good English, his French accent, revealing the hint of a slight American twang.

Our new friend turns out to be Pierre Junot, a member of the village commune, the town council, voted in each year to help the mayor with village matters. Due to his ability to speak English, the mayor has suggested he might call and invite us to the *Amicale Laique*, a sort of umbrella organisation for evening classes of all kinds. Monsieur Junot, it turns out, organises a language class there, for both French and English speakers, giving them an opportunity to get together and share their language and culture.

In conversation we soon find Pierre to be a kind and gently spoken man; he explains he learnt his English while serving with the French Navy in America, which would explain his accent and his upright naval stature. Immediately we find ourselves warming to this gentle, friendly man, who explains his wife also speaks a little English, having worked as a bilingual secretary when she was younger.

Not wanting to intrude, Pierre is happy to leave us with the date of the first class of the new year and the venue in Petit-Villefranche. As he turns to go, he kindly offers to take us along on the first night and we happily agree to get in touch before the class. Waving goodbye, he finally takes his leave stage right, with a casual flick of his quiff and the gentle smile of a matinee idol.

Inside, looking at the clock, I realise there is just enough time to put the white bag containing the turkey in the fridge and prepare a quick lunch of pâté, cheese and fresh crusty bread, before heading to Angoulême to meet Katie off the TGV, which gets in at 3.32pm precisely.

The half-hour journey to Angoulême passes through the rolling fields of the Charentais countryside, stark and bare in their winter hibernation, they stretch out towards the horizon. The vast beauty and silent emptiness of the landscape, leaves me wondering what it will be like in the heat of summer, when the sunflowers turn their huge heads towards the sun and colour is everywhere.

Approaching Angoulême, where it sits on its high rocky precipice, surrounded by old fortified walls and skirted all around by colourful terraced houses descending the steep incline, we disappear into a tunnel in the direction of the train station. Finding a parking space outside, it's time to abandon the car and eager to be in time to greet Katie on the busy platform, we head for the entrance and take our place next to the many colourful figures, wrapped up warm against the cold, as they await the arrival of loved ones home for Christmas.

Right on time, at exactly 3.32pm, the thundering noise of the huge train fills the station, as it draws up on the platform. Our eyes search anxiously, as the doors fly open and the multitudes pour out. There is no sign of Katie anywhere and starting to walk the length of the train we realise just how long it is!

Finally, three carriages from the end, the familiar sight of our daughter, stepping from the train, fills us with delight. Still dressed in Parisian high fashion, she steps into another world. A countryside that is still at least twenty years behind life in the big city, but is waiting to envelop her with open arms, into its relaxed pace of life. "Hi Mum and Dad, happy Christmas!" We hug each other tightly, before heading home to enjoy a quiet Christmas, before the New Year revellers descend!

Christmas Day passes quietly in the old presbytery, except that is for a rather shrill scream emitted by myself at around 9.00am, as I open the white plastic carrier bag from monsieur Bernard. Peering inside to admire my luxury free-range turkey, I certainly don't expect the luxury free-range turkey to be staring admiringly back at me. I don't know which of us looked more surprised, although I didn't hang around long enough to find out! Later that morning, Ron is forced to take on the role of executioner, as our new kitchen is witness to scenes reminiscent of the French Revolution.

By the evening of the 29th, the presbytery sits quietly under a starry sky. Christmas over, Katie and I have just finished preparing rooms for our guests, which no doubt will be fine, until they turn on the lights and realise the decor is definitely more shabby than chic. In the kitchen, however, a welcoming table has been laid with wine and savouries and in his basket Murphy slumbers, unaware of the imminent arrival of our New Year revellers.

At around eight o'clock, an old French Peugeot pulls up at the foot of the steps and out pour five rather excitable twenty-somethings, glad to be released from a cramped car after their long journey from Paris. Katie, scurrying down the steps to greet them disappears in a flurry of kisses and cries of "Ça va?" The peaceful atmosphere of the presbytery slowly evaporates into the cold night air, as the New Year celebrations begin!

First up the steps is Claudine, an actress studying theatre in Paris. Originally from Provence, she is the daughter of a French mother and an English father; greeting us in perfect English and with all the charisma of someone destined for the stage, she is closely followed by Stephan, a student of architecture also based in Paris. Stephan is tall and handsome and comes from the French-speaking part of Geneva, where he has been educated at an international school; he also greets us in perfect English.

Bringing up the rear are Adeline and Gilbert, a French couple from Angers in the heart of the Loire Valley; they have been going out together for just over a year and are both studying and working in Paris. They speak very little English and greet us warmly in French. Finally, as Olivier locks up the car and joins us, it's as if the house breaths a sigh of relief, its walls once again absorbing the familiar sound of the French language, quietly echo the history of by gone years.

In no time everyone is seated around the kitchen table and the buzz of conversation, is only punctuated by the popping of wine corks and the sound of laughter. I begin to realise Katie was right - what a way to start our first year in France, with these lovely young people, unwittingly sharing with us their joie de vivre and giving us at the same time, an insight into French family life.

The conversation soon turns to their plans for New Year's Eve. It seems Ron and I are to be treated to a night of true French gastronomy, as they all try to outdo each other, preparing courses designed to display their cooking skills and also to highlight the produce of their regions. I can't help but think I haven't met any young people of a similar age back home with the same interest in food. Normally, the very thought of spending New Year's Eve with a friend's parents would send them scurrying off to the nearest night club, never mind slogging over a hot stove!

By eleven o'clock Ron and I are happy to retire to bed and we leave the conversation as they begin an animated debate on the best time of year to enjoy oysters. Upstairs we struggle with the makeshift bathroom yet again, before climbing into bed and disappearing under the toile duvet. We are just about to drift off, when the bedroom door opens and the first of our guests appear in the doorway. "Excusez-moi, madame Kennedy," they whisper, as they slip into our room and head for the bathroom. This process is repeated six times as Ron and I look on from under the duvet, smiling politely as they pass.

It hadn't occurred to me that Katie would omit to advise them there was a toilet and wash-hand basin off the kitchen. Mind you, none of the options are up to much, but they were warned that our facilities were basic, to say the least! Eventually the final guests file past in their pyjamas and Ron and I drift off to sleep, feeling already, we have gotten to know our friends - rather more intimately than we had expected!

The day of the 30th quickly becomes one long food-shopping ordeal, as Ron and I help ferry our budding chefs between local markets and vast food outlets like Géant and Intermarché. Everywhere food is prodded, perused and rejected until satisfied they have obtained the best possible ingredients, the items finally make it into the shopping trolley.

Their dedication to the task is admirable, although by now Ron and I would happily settle for a glass of red and some steak frîtes! I do my best, however, to keep his spirits up as we wait in yet another queue, this time at the meat counter, where I have been instructed to purchase eight cailles, or quail, as they are known in English. Looking at Ron I can read his mind, as he questions to himself the possibility of there actually being much meat on the tiny birds, but I assure him the taste will make up for any lack of substance.

Finally returning around six in the evening, we carry the endless supply of bags from the car and proceed like a line of worker ants to ferry them up the steps and into the kitchen. Above us our breath forms clouds of mist that hang in the night air, a testimony to our gargantuan efforts.

Inside the warm kitchen we pack everything into the fridge and eventually gathering around the kitchen table, crack open a bottle of red. Everyone chats enthusiastically about their cooking plans for the next day as I rustle up a simple pasta dish, reluctant to join in what is fast becoming the New Year's edition of Master Chef!

The morning of the festivities eventually dawns bright and crisp and after everyone has negotiated the rudimentary washing facilities, it is obvious the place to be is the kitchen - thank goodness Ron and I made the mad dash to Bordeaux, I think to myself, or there would be no point in gathering there at all! As it is, I watch anxiously as chopping gets underway, unable to stop myself feeling rather fearful for my new beech worktops!

Before I know it, I am wrist-deep, in a sink full of mussels and find myself bringing to mind Katie's words, "Don't worry Mum, we will do all the cooking, you and dad can put your feet up." Well, so far I haven't been asked to do any cooking or to put my feet up, but it is obvious I haven't been ruled out on the preparation front, as I wrestle the beards off masses of black, shiny shellfish.

The chat however is mighty and laughter soon compensates for a bit of hard work. As it happens I am learning as I go and it's not long before I am promoted to the preparation of langoustines. Being an animal lover, this is something I have avoided up to now, but being in France amongst French people, I decide the old motto "When in Rome etc" must be the order of the day and so joining in with gusto, I pull off legs and heads, trying to look debonair, while inside feeling a bit like a mass murderer.

As we chat over the ever-increasing pile of dismembered body parts, the girls discuss what they will wear for the big meal in the evening. I soon realise that they have all brought with them wonderful evening dresses and the men full dinner jackets and accessories! What a spectacle we will make in our glittering dresses, amidst the peeling wallpaper and cracked plasterwork.

Already my new life in France seems like nothing I could have imagined and with great excitement, I run upstairs to search out something exotic, amongst the suitcases of clothes, some of which still remain unopened.

Feeling like a teenager again, I find myself giggling with the girls as we help each other with zips, share make-up and do each other's hair. Claudine looks amazing in a vintage, jewel-encrusted flapper dress, her long hair held in place by a sparkling headband, bedecked with an exotic emerald green feather. Every bit the actress, she bubbles with enthusiasm as we follow her down the stairs, past a waft of amazing smells emanating from the kitchen.

In the living room a long table has been dressed with my beautiful white Irish-linen tablecloth and lit with two silver candelabra. Everywhere young men in full dinner suits, busy themselves preparing the room for the evening's festivities. Ron and I can just look on in amazement, as our old presbytery is transformed before our eyes into a fairytale banqueting hall. Only Katie with her boundless enthusiasm for life and her love for her mum and dad, could have dreamt up such a start to our first year in France.

As the night goes on, the peeling wallpaper is lost in the flickering candlelight. Around the table, Katie and Olivier introduce each new course as it arrives and after a tasting, there is a round of applause for the couple responsible. I brace myself for my first experience of an oyster, and put my head back to be amazed by the cool, salty taste of the sea that slips effortlessly down my throat.

Each course appears magically before us and Ron is amazed at the flavour of the *cailles* smothered in their rich jus and the mouth-watering pan-fried foie gras, which Olivier serves with such enthusiasm.

The night is filled with laughter, new friends and new flavours. Finally at two minutes to midnight, we open the window to the street outside and link arms around the table. At the stroke of midnight the church bells in the village square ring in the new year and around the table Ron, Katie and I teach our enthusiastic French companions the words of "Auld Lang Syne".

Chapter Seven

A Warm Welcome at the, 'Salle des Fêtes'

We are well into the month of January now and this morning took delivery of our long-awaited dishwasher. Memories of the wonderful New Year celebrations, still linger in our minds and with the arrival of the dishwasher, I muse over the fact that our young guests were indeed talented cooks, but perhaps less talented in the washing-up department!

With all the festivities well behind us, work on the presbytery is getting underway. Ron and I have created a very important notebook to record our expenditure, as we begin to engage workmen and buy materials. There have been long discussions, as to where we could create a family bathroom and we have finally decided on the smaller of the two bedrooms at the front of the house. This room with its high ceiling and old marble fireplace is an ample space and should make a really grand *salle de bain*. The fact that it is almost above the downstairs toilet in the utility room makes it a perfect choice, with plumbing close at hand.

It's while thumbing through *les pages jaunes,* the French equivalent of our yellow pages, looking for plumbers, that our concentration is broken by a fracas in the hallway. Murphy, having sensed an imminent invasion, is barking and jumping madly at the letterbox, a ritual normally reserved for the postman, but on this occasion the time of day is wrong. Quickly intervening, before the protruding item is ripped to shreds, I rescue it and returning to the living room, muse to myself on the bravery of the messenger responsible, as Ron hasn't yet got round to removing a rather rusty sign next to the door, declaring '*Chien Mechant*' or dangerous dog!

On closer inspection the offending item appears to be an invitation from the mayor to all villagers, requesting our attendance at the *Salle des Fêtes* on the forthcoming Saturday at noon. The mayor is to give his annual speech, summing up the last year in Saint-Allier and outlining his plans for the forthcoming one. Festivities are to be preceded by aperitifs.

Getting together around the kitchen table, we reread the invitation, checking our translation is correct. Our feelings are a mixture of excitement and anticipation. This will be the first time we are actually going to meet everyone from the village and are aware we will stand out as *les étrangers* or foreigners. It is the opportunity we have been waiting for however, and we agree it is to be grasped with both hands, as we throw ourselves into our new life.

Saturday morning arrives and as the clock heads towards noon, there is a definite stirring in the village. From nowhere people spill out into the street and as if lured by some invisible Pied Piper, snake their way up through the narrow winding pathways towards the *Salle des Fêtes*. Watching from the window, Ron and I agree the moment has arrived and slipping quietly out the front door, follow the crowd, up the steep incline, arriving at the *Salle des Fêtes* in good time for the meeting.

The mayor is standing in the doorway with an attractive woman in her forties, whom he introduces as his wife Danielle. Their greeting is warm and welcoming and amidst the crowds he manages to point us towards a young lady with a tray of aperitifs, before leaving us to resume his duties.

Helping myself to a glass of *pineau*, the local drink preferred by the ladies of the Charente, I stick close to Ron, knowing that his French will be vital, should I be introduced to anyone. The room is filling up and the buzz of the French language is everywhere. I notice Ron sipping gingerly at a glass of cognac. Although early in the day for such firewater, the men of the Charente take it in their stride, as they reach for their second and third glass. I think to myself, perhaps Ron should have gone into some kind of training, if he is not to be legless before the mayor's speech!

The *Salle des Fêtes* itself is a relatively new building, bright and sunny with a shiny wooden floor. At the front of the room a long table sits on a raised platform, no doubt for the mayor and members of his committee. In the middle of the platform a silver microphone takes centre stage, connected to an impressive set of speakers, while on the floor below tables are laid end to end in a crescent shape, to accommodate the villagers as they follow proceedings.

Taking in the surroundings, I am aware of a friendly figure approaching through the crowds and recognise the handsome face of Pierre Junot, as he greets us with his gentle smile. He is eager to introduce his wife Marie, a petite lady in her early sixties. She is perfectly turned out, with an air of Parisian chic and it strikes me at once, they must have been a very handsome couple in their younger days. As I get talking to Marie, she is eager to try out her English, which I soon realise is rather rusty to say the least, but with my French being much the same, our eagerness to get to know each other soon bridges the language barrier and inside I sense this is the start of a lovely friendship.

Pierre goes on to introduce several other villagers, including a monsieur Gilbert Musson. Gilbert, it turns out, is the local plumber and Pierre is eager to impress upon us the quality of his workmanship, using words like '*artisanal*' to describe his dedication to the creation of sanitary perfection. Just as the mayor begins to test the microphone, Ronnie manages to agree a meeting at the presbytery with monsieur Musson for the following Monday morning and with a smile and "à bientôt" the rendezvous is agreed.

As we take our seats, the mayor, looking as handsome as ever, in a rather dapper navy-blue blazer and grey twill trousers, greets the villagers and thanks every one for coming along. He wastes no time confidently launching into his speech, as he covers the events of the past year and outlines his plans for the forthcoming one. Straining to follow, I listen intently and somehow manage to keep up with proceedings reasonably well.

He is just explaining that this year they look forward to finishing the '*Parc des Boules*', which is being created behind the church and the renovation of the old *lavoir*, or washhouse, on the same site. This will obviously be a great addition to the village, creating a really pretty recreation area for all the family. The amusing thing being, as we are later to discover, that it is the proceedings from the sale of the presbytery, by the commune to ourselves, that has provided the funds to complete this project!

As the mayor's speech draws to a close, to our surprise and delight, we hear our names amongst the stream of French and realise the mayor is introducing us to our fellow villagers. With a broad smile he encourages us to stand up and make ourselves known to everybody, which we do rather shyly, only to be met by a ripple of applause from our wonderful neighbours. If we ever wondered whether we would be accepted in Saint-Allier, we have no doubts now and as we sit down Ron and I look at each other and inside we couldn't feel happier.

The proceedings finally come to an end, as the mayor wishes us all a happy and prosperous New Year, leaving the stage to more enthusiastic applause. Rising from our seats we turn around to head home, only to be met by a couple obviously keen to make themselves known to us. A hand is outstretched by a smallish gentleman, very fit looking with steely-grey hair and bright, eager blue eyes, he introduces himself as Henri Buisson and proudly announces he is our next-door neighbour.

Looking to the left of Henri, our eyes are drawn upwards to the face of his wife, a considerably younger woman and much taller than Henri; she also is smiling broadly. There follows an animated conversation, as we all get to know each other. It turns out Henri has been married before, as he tells us he has a daughter of three called Amelie and two older boys from his first marriage. He proudly announces his second wife - Chantal is 15 years his junior, a fact that he relates with some relish and goes on to say how they met through judo, a sport where they have both achieved black-belt status.

Heading home down the winding lanes towards the presbytery, we eagerly share our thoughts on all the new characters we have met, filling each other in on any snippets of news the other might have missed. We chat about the couple that own the *boulangerie*, a Madame Édith Lebert and her husband Frank. Édith, a short, rather severe-looking woman in her late fifties, showed a distinct lack of any sense of humour and as for her husband Frank, well let's just say, he may well have been the reason why.

Frank, a heavily set figure with a mass of thick unruly black hair, which not only sprouted from his head but also from his chin in the form of a massive black beard, revealed a distinct personality bypass, only occasionally grumping from within the beard in a rather inaudible fashion. They didn't exactly inspire one to rush to the *boulangerie* and become one of their regulars! Indeed it is true to say, many of our new-found friends in the village had admitted they used the *boulangerie* in the next village for this very reason.

It was lovely, however, to have met our neighbours Henri and Chantal, who have already offered to be of any assistance they can during our renovations. On the other side of the presbytery we have the mayor and his wife Danielle, who have both been so welcoming. Tucked between the two and nestled in the heart of the pretty French village of Saint-Allier, we are really starting to feel an integral part of this little community.

Chapter Eight

Home Alone?

As the next weeks go by, during the long wintry days of January and February, we forge on with our renovations. Looking forward to the warmth of spring, we are happy to put in the effort now, in the hope that as summer arrives, we will be free to relax and take in our new surroundings.

Gilbert Musson has agreed to take on the plumbing work, which he is keen to start towards the end of February, involving the creation of a new family bathroom, the complete refurbishment of the en-suite in the back bedroom and the installation of four new radiators to complete the central heating system.

A plumpish chap with chubby red cheeks, Gilbert has been a real joy to do business with; nothing seems to be a problem for him. His enthusiasm for plumbing, we discover, is only matched by his passion for collecting rare whiskies and Ron enjoys introducing him to the delights of some of our Irish varieties.

With only two weeks to go now, until monsieur Noel is to start the rewiring, which will involve a massive upheaval, Ron and I find ourselves coming back to a plan we had at the back of our minds ever since we moved in. Having read much advice about how to make a successful move to France, we are aware that inviting the neighbours in for aperitifs is a really good way to extend the hand of friendship and get to know everyone.

It is while sitting around the open fire in the living room, discussing the said venture over a glass of wine, that a phone call from our son Richard, confirms the timing for our *soirée* couldn't be better. He plans to arrive for a long weekend at the beginning of February, just the week before monsieur Noel is due to start. It will be the first time he and his partner, Eadaoin, have seen the presbytery and the thought that they would be here to help with the entertaining is an added bonus, especially as Richard is a fluent French speaker.

And so our plan begins to come together. While rummaging around the local newsagent in Petit-Villefranche, I come across some printed invitation cards that appear to be perfect. It is obvious that the French enjoy throwing *soirées*, as there is quite a selection to choose from and I finally decide on a suitable pack of ten and head for the cash desk.

Back home we carefully fill out the cards, personalising those for the mayor and his wife, along with our neighbours on the other side, Henri and Chantal Buisson. The remaining cards we leave as an open invitation, having of course no idea who will receive them, but addressing the envelopes to the ten houses that make up our little corner of the village. Looking at the neat pile on the table in front of us, we glance at each other and agree, that we can't imagine what people will think when the invitations arrive through their doors. Let's hope they are as keen to meet us as we are to get to know them!

The next morning, wrapped up against a keen frost, we pop the lead on Murphy and pull the heavy front door of the presbytery behind us as we step out into the street. There is no one about, which we both agree is the perfect scenario for our covert operation to deliver the invitations, not wishing to have to start explaining in French what we are up to!

The heavy ancient doors of the village houses look like they have hung there for centuries; behind some, one can hear the bustle of family life and others reveal a cavernous darkness inside, visible through gaping letterboxes. In the icy mist our breath hangs in the air, emphasising the stillness of our little community, where all life as we have come to realise, appears to play out behind closed doors, leading one to believe falsely, that the place is deserted.

Finally, posting the last invitation through a door marked 'Chien Méchant', we beat a hasty retreat to the sound of some rather vicious growling. Let's hope our delivery isn't torn to shreds before the homeowner has had time to consider our invitation!

Over the next few days, we are to be found in our local Intermarché alcohol section, like a couple of secret drinkers, trying to judge exactly how much and what sort of aperitifs our guests will expect. We decide to go with what we know to be the local tipple, from our visit to the Salle des Fêtes, that is pineau for the ladies and Ricard or whiskey for the men.

While we are here we stock up on nibbles, to which a whole aisle in the supermarket has been allocated, proving yet again, the importance of the *Apéritif* or *Apéro*, as an integral part of French country life. Some local cheeses to accompany these finally complete our shop and we head home to stock up our drinks cabinet in preparation for Friday evening at 7pm, when our hopes are high that we can forge some kind of 'entente cordiale', with our new French neighbours!

On a cold misty Wednesday evening, we pick Richard and Eadaoin up from the airport at Bergerac, an hour-long drive both ways, with fog lights full on; but the time is filled catching up with their lives and sharing our adventures so far. Inside the warmth of the car, I prepare them again for the fact that life at the presbytery is still pretty primitive, explaining the bathroom situation, while advising cautious use of the electrics! I needn't have worried, however, as both having survived student digs are well used to roughing it.

Katie joins us on Friday morning, unable to resist a chance to get together with her brother. It feels so good to hear the house filled with the familiar sounds of family life. I think to myself having both my children together under the same roof is a rare opportunity these days. Empty nest syndrome had unfortunately coincided with Ron's illness, consolidating a feeling of loss that has encompassed us both over the last decade. But this is no time for dwelling on the past, as we prepare to take another giant step into the future and I busy myself creating an attractive table to welcome our new French friends.

Glancing at the clock, it's 6.50 just ten minutes to go and the scene for our *soirée* is set. Gathered together in the dining room, we are all feeling nervous. Will anyone turn up? Perhaps only one or two will come and our table, creaking under its spread of *Apéro* delights, will stand out starkly, a monument to lack of interest from our new foreign neighbours.

"Right mum, who's for a glass of wine?" Richard manages to break the tension of the moment with the pop of a wine cork and the glug of ruby red liquid filling our waiting glasses. It may not be the tipple of choice for our neighbours, who prefer to enjoy the said beverage with meals, but as Richard announces a toast, "To mum and dad and their new life in France!" it just hits the spot. The next ten minutes are taken up with random joke telling, encouraged by the rapid consumption of the said beverage, mixed with an undercurrent of nervous tension.

Seven o'clock comes and goes. Peering out into the street, it's as though all human life has been beamed to another planet. If a ball of tumbleweed were to roll down the main street, it couldn't look more deserted. Back in the room, spirits are beginning to flag. Just as the jokes start to fall flat and hopes along with them, the doorbell rings, fifteen minutes later than expected. At least someone has taken up our invitation. A bit embarrassing though, I think to myself, with so much on the table and perhaps one lone couple, what on earth will we talk about?

Wrestling with the old front door, it finally opens to reveal the street; now filled with what I can only describe as a throng of people and right at the front stands the mayor, hardly visible behind a huge bunch of fresh flowers! "*Bienvenue à Saint-Allier!*" he declares in a booming voice and the surrounding throng break into a ripple of applause and a loud cheer. Completely overwhelmed, I gesture to them to come in and not needing to be asked twice, they pour into the presbytery enveloping my little family and me in a sea of handshakes and kisses.

Over the next hour we manage to put names to many of the faces. Danielle, the mayor's wife, slim and attractive, is deep in conversation with Katie, as I entertain little Amèlie, the three-year-old daughter of our neighbours, Henri and Chantal. Amèlie is intrigued by me, probably as my efforts at French lead her to believe I can't be much older than herself!

From the house across the road we have Marie, a stout lady, perhaps in her late seventies, who it turns out was the housekeeper in the presbytery, when the priest was still alive. Marie is blessed with a jolly sense of humour and is being egged on mercilessly, by Young Jacques Reneau. Young Jacques, as he is referred to by all present, would be in his early forties and lives on the other side of the lane that leads to the back of the presbytery; he is neighbour to Old Jacques, who in his early eighties, is a former Tour de France cyclist and is as fit as a fiddle! It appears the two Jacques's are always referred to as young and old respectively, to avoid any confusion.

Offering a tray of pineaus to the ladies, I meet Inès, who is newly married to Young Jacques. I soon work out it is a second marriage for Jacques, but the first for Inès. She strikes me as a quiet, gentle woman and obviously quite in love with the vivacious Young Jacques, who as we speak is encouraging Marie to demonstrate her dancing prowess, which in her exuberance reveals a glimpse of long johns and suspenders, throwing the whole room into peals of laughter!

Finally, the mayor is the first to wish us "Bonne Soirée" and the others gradually follow suit, bidding us good night with the customary three kisses. We can't help but feel accepted and welcomed by our new neighbours, who leave with promises of assistance with everything from tree felling by our neighbour Henri, to Old Jacques who promises to prune our vines, as he has done at the presbytery for as long as he can remember.

Closing the door on the last of our guests, we get our first chance to compare notes and with a group hug and a communal sigh of relief, we all agree it couldn't have gone better!

Chapter Nine

Henri and His Amazing 'bête'

The months of February and March are enveloped in a shroud of plaster dust and swallowed up by the deafening noise of a Kango drill as the electricians track the walls. Ron and I survive, rather than flourish, employed in an endless round of cleaning, in a vain attempt to preserve what furnishings we have. When the dust begins to settle, monsieur Musson has transformed the front bedroom into a beautiful family bathroom, not yet tiled or finished but functional and everywhere efficient new switches, plugs and sockets provide electricity without the imminent risk of electrocution! Outside our dust-filled world, unbeknown to us, spring has been creeping up; everywhere there is the smell of new growth in the air and often a gentle warmth bathes the landscape, whispering of heat to come.

Sitting with a cup of coffee in my hand, on the smooth, worn top step, at the front of the presbytery and looking out over the park, to the hills beyond, I can't believe this is our home. I run my hand over the one-hundred-year-old steps, worn by the feet of so many parishioners, who came here in the past to seek counsel from the priest. What were their stories? What solace did they find in this place? One of the villagers told me the presence of the cross above the door into the street meant there would be food and respite here for lonely travellers and jokingly suggested we might find a queue there some morning!

Smiling to myself at the thought, out of the corner of my eye I detect a movement to the left of the old barn. Someone is in the garden and looking round for Ronnie, I soon realise he is nowhere to be seen. Aware of my limited French, I bravely take the bull by the horns and head down the garden towards the furtive figure of an old man in denim dungarees. Approaching, I recognise our visitor from the night of the *soirée* - it's Old Jacques and he is busily pruning away at our vines.

"*Bonjour Jacques. Ça va*?" I am quick with the customary greeting, but wonder inside, where I go from here. I needn't have worried, however, Jacques is much too engrossed in his pruning and only stops to explain what he is doing. Nodding knowingly as he describes with passion the art of vine pruning, he promises me a fine harvest of grapes to come and looking into his lovely old face, wrinkled and weathered by years under the hot sun, I find myself entranced by the dark brown eyes full of warmth and friendship. Eventually taking my leave, I wish him "Bonne chance!" with his labours and leave him happy in his work, as I make my way back up the garden.

Deep in thought, I can't help but contrast my life now with the years living in suburban Belfast, where neighbours hide behind closed doors and are only perceivable by the twitch of a curtain. Suspicious of strangers and subdued by a dull grey climate.

As I reach the steps, I am stopped in my tracks by a hearty "Bonjour!" and looking back, spot Henri leaning on the gate, with little Amèlie by his side. To my relief Ron appears at the top of the steps and we go down together for a friendly chat. Henri reminds us of his promise to help cut back the two enormous yew trees in front of the presbytery, one on either side of the entrance.

They were most likely planted at the same time as the building was constructed, which would make them over one hundred years old and almost as tall as the house itself. Where they stand, they block out a lot of light from the front of the house and I would imagine cast a shadow across Henri's garden, possibly blocking light to his house too.

He mentions he has his brother's chainsaw at the moment and asks if we would be free this afternoon to tackle the job. Our eyes look upwards towards the top of the towering trees and simultaneously think, what has Henri in mind? Which of us is climbing to the top with a chainsaw? Anyway the deal is sealed over a glass of pastis, shared in Henri's kitchen, before we all adjourn for lunch in our respective houses.

A few hours later the peace of the presbytery is rocked by loud knocking on the door, which when opened reveals Henri, his young wife Chantal, Amèlie and their large dog, Plato. Before we can '*dit bonjour*', Murphy takes one look at Plato and has him down as a marauding invader. Holding him back, still barking and displaying rather a large number of teeth, Ron manages to wrestle him into the living room and slams the door shut.

We complete our greetings, but on no occasion during the afternoon do our French neighbours suggest returning Plato to his own abode, instead he spends his time roaming around the garden marking his territory, while Murphy is confined to barracks. It is the start of an arch-rivalry between the two, which is confirmed when Murphy finally gets to read the said messages, placed carefully on the base of each tree, in what of course, is Murphy's territory!

Back in the garden however, discussion is underway on how best to tackle the two enormous arboreal specimens. Thankfully Henri has warned no one to touch the chainsaw, (not that there was a great queue forming there anyway!) and has indicated he will climb the trees himself, slinging the '*bête*', as he likes to refer to it, over his shoulder.

I detect a certain amount of macho muscle-flexing and showing off, mostly directed at his young wife, Chantal, who seems duly impressed. In fact Henri on several occasions, has made reference to the fact that he is the proud possessor of, "*beaucoup de musculation*" or lots of muscles. I can see Ron thinking, if this is what it takes to impress a much younger wife, he would rather opt for the older model, requiring a lot less effort!

Before we can say "*Bonne chance!*", Henri, like a monkey, has leapt into the first tree and starts to climb. With the chainsaw strapped to his back, his hands are freed up and he makes fast progress, until soon he is perched high above us, where the trunk of the tree separates out into heavy boughs and branches.

As we gaze admiringly upwards he leans nonchalantly back, frees both hands and proceeds to wrench the starting cord of the chainsaw violently, until on the third occasion, it roars into life. Holding it above his head in a triumphal gesture and with a wide grin from ear to ear, he demonstrates his best impression of a cross between Tarzan and Rambo!

Skilfully he saws through the branches and as they fall to the ground, we are instructed to grab hold and drag them to the bottom of the garden, where eventually, they are destined to form part of an enormous bonfire. As he tackles some of the biggest boughs, we tie a heavy rope around them, so they avoid the house as they fall. Ron, Chantal and I, taking the strain, pull them to one side, where our hero, Henri, has promised to chop them into logs for the winter.

Two hours later the first tree finished, we take a break and bringing out a tray of ice-cold beers, everyone takes a well-earned rest. The job is a good one and our old yew tree is now less than half its original height and finished in a neat, rotund shape. Running inside to the living room and then to the bedroom above, I am greeted by sun-filled rooms, that haven't enjoyed the light of day for many years and looking across to Henri's garden bathed in golden light, I call from the bedroom window, "*Il y a plus de lumière maintenant, chez-toi aussi!*" Our labours are rewarded ten times over.

Back in the garden the whole operation begins again in earnest and light is almost fading by the time Henri descends from the second tree, for the last time. His skin glistens with sweat and his muscles ripple, as he lowers the '*bête*' to the ground. Ron and I burst into spontaneous applause and Chantal looks on in admiration, eyes only for her hero!

It is impossible to thank Henri enough, we could never have afforded a professional tree feller and as the two lovebirds head off hand in hand, closely followed by Amèlie and Plato, Ron and I release the dejected Murphy and set about clearing as much of the remaining branches as we can to the now enormous bonfire.

A week of cooler but dry weather later, Ron, Murphy and I gather at the bottom of the garden in the fading light and apply a match to some scrunched-up newspapers wedged at the base of the huge bonfire. The papers catch immediately, curling and emitting sparks that float high into the evening air, dancing like fireflies, while Murphy jumps in vain to catch them. Meanwhile, the scorched wood crackles and bursts into flames, licking hungrily upwards and before we can gasp, "*Merde*!" we find ourselves standing next to the towering inferno!

The gentle breeze fans the flames in the direction of Henri's garden, where his precious, if rather dilapidated caravan, rests sleepily on the other side of the bushes. Awoken abruptly from a mesmerised trance, Ron grabs a spade and starts to beat the burning branches down on the side nearest to Henri's holiday home, disappearing momentarily into a cloud of smoke and reappearing coughing and spluttering.

It's us against the elements and the game is on. Never have we felt so alive or so connected to the earth beneath us. Living in the moment, all the worries of the past years disappear in the clouds of smoke. Ron shouts to throw some more branches onto the fire as we gain control of its direction and we are able to stand back and look on with respect at the power of Mother Nature. Glancing over at Ron in the fading light, his face aglow from the heat of the fire and his hair filled with the smell of wood smoke, I realise I am witnessing the healing power of our new life, on the man I love.

Chapter Ten

Market Day: A Horsey Affair!

Having spent the last months on our dusty building site, Wednesdays have come and gone like any other, with the only hint of market day being the increase in traffic passing through our little village, on its way to Petit-Villefranche. My intention on many a winter's morning had been to foray out and investigate, but with artisans arriving and requiring our presence on site all day, we simply continued to shop in the same fashion as we had back home, with a weekly visit to our local supermarket.

Strangely enough, it is a trip to the vet with Murphy that becomes the impetus for our early rise this morning and our plan to pay a visit to the weekly market, just five minutes away, in the neighbouring village of Petit-Villefranche. Perhaps I should explain, before going any further, exactly what I mean.

Murphy, like many Westies, has suffered from skin complaints on and off for much of his life and these have flared up again, causing him to chew his paws until they are raw and sore. Each time this happens, there comes a point when, as owners, we can no longer sit back and watch him suffer. So forced to search out the nearest vet, we are sadly reminded of our unfortunate omission to take out pet insurance!

On this occasion it was a Monsieur Karl van de Burren, a Dutch vet, who had the pleasure of relieving us of our hard-earned savings. Arriving for our rendezvous at 10.30am on Monday morning, I drew up in front of his rather plush, glass-fronted establishment, set back from the road, amidst leafy, well-kept gardens and jumping out of the car, led a dejected-looking Murphy into the light and airy reception area.

It was hard, at this point, to work out if the dejected look was due to his sore paws or his innate ability to recognise a veterinary establishment at fifty paces. On reflection I suspect it was the latter.

Finally appearing, Monsieur Van de Burren greeted us in perfect English and invited me to pop Murphy onto the table, where he would proceed with his examination. Despite some rather evil growling from the patient, the examination is eventually complete and as expected, his findings are consistent with those of previous vets back home.

Releasing a deep sigh, while leaning back nonchalantly against the adjacent work surface, he eventually enlightens us with his medical expertise: "In my opinion, it is most likely a skin allergy brought on by years of in-breeding designed to achieve the perfect white coat typical of the breed." Grinning somewhat smugly to himself, he further advises, "Next time you find yourselves investing in a pet, I would recommend a mongrel, if not, then at least a very large insurance policy."

Well, we have been down the allergy route before, having tried just about every expensive dog food, scientifically proven to minimise the allergic reaction, but Monsieur van de Burren's solution was something new.

"Horse meat! That is the answer!" and slipping into French with a distinctly Dutch accent, he enthusiastically declares, "*C'est merveilleux!*" Apparently, according to our esteemed vet, it is one of the few types of meat proven to be completely allergy free and he swears by it. I, on the other hand, am slightly taken aback, having made a conscious decision on behalf of my family and myself, not to add any further species of animal to those we already reluctantly consume.

Returning to the car just five minutes later, I found myself clutching a tube of seriously expensive anti-inflammatory ointment, a solution to be added to Murphy's bath water, which will involve us all in a daily soaking and a note directing me to Madame Pivot, who runs a stall at the Wednesday market, selling horse meat.

Looking out the window now, the park is bathed in a watery sunlight and the hills beyond wear a blanket of early morning mist. At the foot of the steps, Ron climbs into the car, his breath hanging in the air, a sign that temperatures in the Charente at this time of the year don't always reflect the arrival of spring.

Popping Murphy into his basket by the radiator, I leave him to attend to his irritating paws, while I run down the steps and join my husband in the car. Setting off on our mission to explore the market and locate Madame Pivot, we pass through the gates and along the lane, until arriving at the exit; we join the long line of traffic, all heading in the same direction.

Arriving at the little town, our usual route to the *centre ville* is closed off and we are directed around the periphery to a large car park just behind the main street. It is early, but the car park is full and already people are returning to their vehicles, laden down with bags of fresh vegetables, baguettes and plants for the garden. All around the atmosphere is vibrant. Our sleepy little town, nestling in the shadow of the Château, has been transformed into a bustling hub of activity and Ron and I can't wait to get out there and do some exploring.

Buttoning up my jacket and reaching for Ron's hand, together we join the sea of humanity, heading in the direction of the town square. Everywhere, the air is filled with the chatter of locals catching up with old friends, while nearby, music rising through the crowd, mixes with the smell of roasting chickens on an adjacent spit.

Looking down the main street in both directions, either side of the road is filled with colourful stalls, their merchandise spilling over unto the pavement in front of them. It would appear hoards of people have been gathering here each Wednesday, while Ron and I, oblivious to the popularity of our nearby town, have been hibernating, totally absorbed in our renovation project, often imagining ourselves to be in the middle of nowhere!

How wrong could we have been? Our choice of Saint-Allier has turned out, rather by luck than design, to be geographically perfect. Five minutes from a busy market town and thirty minutes from a major city on the TGV line, while at the heart of a thriving tourist region.

Easing our way through the busy throng to a nearby stall, bedecked in the colourful, flowery house coats, as worn by all self respecting ' *femmes de ménages*', we begin to feel like the luckiest people alive, having more or less chosen the place by sticking a pin in the map!

Perusing the stall, I come to the conclusion I am neither old enough, nor French enough yet, to adopt the uniform of the 'flowery wrap-around house coat' and navigating our way back through a crowd of overexcited French housewives, all intent on getting their hands on the latest model, we head back towards the centre of the road, where the flow of bodies moves effortlessly towards the town square.

Passing a long cheese stall on our left, just before the bridge, my attention is drawn to a pleasant lady dressed in a white apron. She holds out a tray of cheeses enquiring, "*Vous pouvez les essayer, Madame*." An offer we find impossible to resist and as a result, the next ten minutes are spent oblivious of the surrounding chaos, tasting and discussing the merits of the various *fromages*. Rejoining the throng, we finally leave with a selection of our favourites for lunch later.

Crossing the bridge up ahead, Ron, who never misses a thing, spots the words, '*Viande Chevaline*', written in large, blue letters across the top of a van parked neatly between two stalls and, as we draw closer the words: '*Propriètaire, Madame Pivot*', confirm we have arrived at our destination.

Approaching an open window at the side of the van, we encounter Madame, a small but wiry lady of indiscernible age, whose bright, beady eyes are swift to spot our curiosity as she enquires, " *Puis-je vous aider*?"

The story, being slightly complicated, is left to Ron to explain - how our unfortunate pet's medical history has lead us to her stall today. Eventually, with the mention of Monsieur Van de Burren, her face finally reveals the penny has dropped and she knows exactly what we require. Apparently, the vet sends a regular stream of customers her way, with his belief in her merchandise seemingly being the cure for most things!

In the interior of the van, Madame fills a bag with what look like leftover pieces of meat and weighing the same, pops them in a bag, in return for a minimal payment. Smiling, she hands over the package, wishing our unfortunate pet " *Bonne sante*!"

Leaving the stall, the story of *Black Beauty* flashes briefly across my mind and I make a mental effort to accept, if I am going to eat a cow, I can't complain about cooking horse for the dog. Being an animal lover, I have for a long time wrestled with the idea of becoming a vegetarian, but I do enjoy meat and living in France hasn't made the choice any easier, so for the meantime I remain on the meat eating side of the fence.

Luckily, the colourful spectacle around me soon banishes any further thoughts of glossy-coated stallions and, passing the estate agent where our adventure first began all those months earlier, we encounter Laurent, enjoying one of his regular coffee breaks, while watching the world go by.

"*Monsieur et Madame Kennedy. Bonjour, vous allez bien*?" Returning his greeting, we enquire how business is at the moment and leaning back in his doorway, while taking another nonchalant puff on his cigarette, he acknowledges it to be slow, but smiles mischievously admitting, "*Mais, pas de problème. Encore, en printemps, les Anglais arriveraient*!"

We share our little joke, with its element of truth, acknowledging that the English have indeed played a big part in the regeneration of towns like Petit-Villefranche. Most of the young people having moved to the city means it's often left to the English to buy up and renovate the subsequently deserted properties.

Leaving Laurent to finish his cigarette, we make our way up to the square, where stalls are crowded around the little fountain and in the corner, tables spill onto the street from the local *bar du marché.*' Ron and I recognise at once an excellent spot to people-watch and, noticing an empty table at the front, are quick to claim our place.

It's not long before we are warming our hands around a hot cup of coffee. Lost in thought, I become engulfed in the noise and smells of the place and sipping my coffee, I can feel myself melt into the colourful atmosphere, like we are being seamlessly absorbed into this little community.

In the crowds that pass, I watch friends greet each other with kisses and look on, as they animatedly share news of their families. On the far side of the square a smart young woman hurries by carrying a huge bunch of flowers whilst balancing a box from the patisserie in her free hand and by the fountain, an elderly lady pauses, letting her little dog lean over for a drink in the clear water.

Leisurely searching the sea of faces gathered around a bric-a-brac stall on the corner, my eye catches a flash of silver-grey hair and at once I recognise the debonair quiff of our good friend, Pierre Junot. It's not long before he spots us and cutting across the square to join us, he pulls up a chair at our table and with the ease of a matinee idol orders, "*Un espresso.*"

As the morning heads towards noon, we chat with our good friend about everything under the sun, looking for all the world like we

74

had been meeting here for years. Finally, Pierre acknowledging that Marie will be sending out a search party soon, bids us a reluctant farewell and with the usual three kisses, joins the now dwindling crowd, whose thoughts are rapidly turning to *déjeuner*.

Back at the car, we have managed to pick up two carrier bags full of fresh vegetables, olives and cold meats since leaving Pierre and pop them safely into the boot, along with Monsieur Van de Burren's bag of 'miracle cure' meat!

Later in the day, as we retire to the *séjour* for the evening, Murphy flops onto the rug at our feet, having just consumed his first bowl of '*Viande de cheval*', while Ron and I contentedly relive our visit to the market. As the evening unfolds, our little dog sleeps the sleep of a contented, well-fed pet, waking only occasionally to lick his paws. Causing me to reflect, it may be some time before the miracle cure finally kicks in.

Chapter eleven

Chez Pierre and Marie

Tuesday evenings find us as usual, sitting around a table in Petit-Villefranche, at our English-French conversation class, chatting animatedly with Jim and Lynn Carter, an English couple from South London. They came to France about a year ago, after Jim suffered a major heart attack, followed by lengthy surgery. It would have been understandable, after such an event, if they had chosen to spend their retirement, five miles from their local hospital in London, but instead this courageous couple, in their late sixties, looked upon the whole thing as a wake-up call.

Jim has a good grasp of French and Lynn, an intelligent woman with an enquiring mind and a kind heart, is never seen without her dictionary; fascinated to be learning something new in later life, she is always the first to ask questions. They now find themselves the proud owners of a beautiful old farmhouse, perched near the top of a hill, just outside Saint-Allier. It boasts magnificent views over the valley below, where in summer the fields are filled with sunflowers.

Seated opposite, are two French ladies, Clemence and Monique. In their mid-fifties, they are always immaculately turned out and have been studying English together for several years. They are reasonably competent in the language, although rather sweetly, their fear of making idiots of themselves generally renders them somewhat reluctant to start a conversation.

Next to Clemence and Monique, are a young English couple, Pauline and Gary, they have little grasp of the French language and no real interest in acquiring one it would seem, but turn up each week with various French documents and household bills, in search of a free translation service!

Completing the class are Pierre and Marie Junot looking as chic as ever. Wendy, an attractive English lady in her mid-sixties, with her husband Harold, who suffers from Parkinson's disease and lastly, a French chap with a huge moustache, who has yet to open his mouth. Finally sitting at the head of the table is our coordinator Brigitte Lambert.

Brigitte insists she is not a teacher and is simply there to guide the conversation with the use of some local newspaper articles. Assertiveness is not one of her best attributes, however, and it is some time before the class gets underway. When it eventually does, her articles are surreptitiously put to one side, as we all reluctantly agree to translate Pauline and Gary's planning application for a new swimming pool!

The class, even with its lack of coordination, is invaluable to Ron and I, as it has allowed us to improve our language skills and has turned out to be a great way to make friends, both French and English. We eventually part company for the night, with an invite for *apéros* at Pierre and Marie's on the following Thursday.

After a busy week, covered in dust from head to toe following yet more sanding and painting, we are glad when Thursday arrives and can scrub up for a well-deserved break. Outside it is a balmy spring day with a gentle breeze, as we head off just before four o'clock in search of Pierre and Marie's house.

The road winds steeply up from the village and as we pass the little cemetery, where we discovered people were living well into their eighties, even a hundred years ago, I find myself wondering if it is the sunshine, the red wine or just the slower pace of life that contributed to their longevity? After all, these people were not rich and their living conditions would have been basic; in a different climate they may not have fared so well. Deep in thought, my mind drifts back to my own homeland, with its bleak weather, where many years ago the Potato Famine, due to blight, claimed the lives of thousands and the average life expectancy would have been so much lower.

Turning the corner, a shaft of bright sunlight jolts me back to reality and Ron points to a tiny group of houses at the end of a winding lane to our left. We are almost there. The car pulls into the centre of the little hamlet and we follow Pierre's directions to the house at the end of the track, with its pale green shutters and beautiful wrought-iron gates. As we pass, the villagers look up from their work - their tranquillity momentarily disturbed, causing a ripple of inquisitiveness to interrupt their purposeful afternoon labours.

Slowly gliding through the gates we arrive in a gravel courtyard, brightly decorated with huge terracotta pots of burgeoning flowers. Around us the garden-walls are shrouded with ivy and everywhere the air is filled with the background hum of crickets and the occasional buzz of a passing insect. Pierre suddenly appears from the barn to our left, looking as dapper as ever. His silver quiff glistening in the sunshine above his delicate tanned features and welcoming smile, still reminiscent of a Hollywood star of bygone years. "*Bonjour mes amis, ça va?*" His welcome is generous and accompanied by three kisses each, making us feel relaxed and happy as we follow him into the house to find Marie.

Inside it is dark and as my eyes readjust, I find myself in the kitchen of this old farmhouse, where modern wood units sit comfortably against the old stonewalls. Everything is held together by antique furniture and stylish elaborate wrought-iron chandeliers, which perfectly marry the old with the new.

Marie greets us with her gentle smile and some more kissing. She is immaculately turned out and although in her sixties, is poised and slim and wears her clothes like a Parisian fashion model. It has not escaped my notice, that in contrast to Britain, where women tend to become invisible in their sixties, France celebrates women of all ages, acknowledging the beauty and serenity of the older woman.

Marie reaches for a tray and suggests we head out to the garden. Following her we are led to an old table next to a huge weeping willow and fall into some comfortable wicker chairs festooned with colourful, soft cushions. On the table Marie places the tray, on which is a delicious-looking *tarte Tatin*, four wine glasses and a rather old bottle of wine, still bearing the dust from many years tucked away in Pierre's cellar.

As Marie cuts the *tarte*, Pierre explains, for this special occasion, he has chosen a bottle of Montbazillac, which has been maturing in his cellar for many years. He goes on to explain it is a speciality of the region. A sweet dessert wine with an unexpected kick! The perfect accompaniment to Marie's *tarte Tatin*. Effortlessly, he uncorks the bottle and pours a small amount of the golden liquid into each of our glasses, for tasting.

The table falls silent for this reverential moment. I lift the glass to my lips and it reflects the bright sunlight into my eyes, as the golden liquid caresses my lips, sliding down my throat; it has the smooth, sweet taste of honey and alcohol, followed by the warming afterglow of a vintage brandy. I pause for a moment savouring its rich aftertaste and then exclaim to Pierre's great delight, "*C'est bon, c'est très bon!*"

As the late afternoon slips by, conversation flows, along with the Montbazillac! Ron and Claude eventually disappear off in the direction of the barn to inspect his woodcutting equipment, leaving Marie and I to sort out the world, as we women do. It's amazing how the language barrier just melts away when the need to communicate takes over. We talk about everything under the sun and I think to myself how much we have in common, even though we come from such different worlds.

Some time later, clearing in the tray, Marie shows me around her home. It is a rambling old place she inherited from Pierre's parents, along with much of the antique furniture, which she cherishes, lovingly running her hand along the smooth, rich mahogany surfaces, as she describes the history behind each piece.

Climbing the stairs behind her, I find myself on a galleried landing, looking down to the dining room below. In front of us, suspended from the ceiling above the dining room, is a huge antique glass chandelier. From the landing, it fills the whole space with a kind of baroque splendour and I can just picture the table below, heavy with food and wine, illuminated by its sparkling incandescence.

There is much to see and stories to be told of those who inhabited this beautiful place in years gone by and I find myself envying this women's connection with the past, that is all around her and leaves her in no doubt, where she fits in time and history.

Opening a drawer, Marie pulls out three huge, old leather-bound scrapbooks and lays them on the bed. She explains how an aunt, working in the fashion industry in Paris around the 1920's, left them to her. Lovingly, she turns the pages to reveal the most exquisite hand-drawn fashion designs, by some of the most famous fashion houses of the *époque*, delicately and expertly executed in pale and faded shades of ink.

The arrival of Ron and Pierre clambering up the wooden stairs, heralds the end of our imaginary stroll down the catwalk and Marie closes the books, tucking them safely back into the old oak chest, until the next time she wishes to step back into the 1920's world of haute couture.

Pierre is eager to show Ron the enormous *grenier* or roof space and Marie and I tag along on the final stage of this magical mystery tour. A short flight of wooden stairs from the landing takes us into this huge space, with full headroom to stand up. The size of the massive oak beams is quite breathtaking and Pierre is proud to inform us they are hundreds of years old.

Everywhere things are covered with old dustsheets and as our hosts pull them back, they explain that all these wonderful antique mirrors, armoires and paintings are family heirlooms, left by previous generations. At this point Ron and I find ourselves wondering, if there is any chance they might be feeling rather top heavy with family heirlooms and would perhaps feel the need to offload some!

I can just imagine how they would look so at home in the old presbytery. It appears however, one can never have too many family heirlooms and it is just unfortunate for us, our ancestors obviously didn't look after things quite so well, or else simply decided to take them with them - seemingly disproving the old adage that one can't!

As specks of dust dance merrily in the shafts of light from the skylight windows, we take our leave of Pierre's attic. Beneath their dustsheets, Marie's treasures lie like sleeping ghosts, left to rest, until the next time they are called upon to give up the secrets of times gone by.

Outside in the warm evening sunshine, we prepare to take our leave. Marie joins us from the kitchen with some fresh fruit from the garden, carefully wrapped in a brown paper bag, for us to take home. After hugs and three kisses each, we agree to meet again, on Tuesday at the language class and climb into the car.

Pulling out of the driveway, our goodbyes are lost in the sound of crunching gravel and as we pass through the little hamlet everywhere is silent, the busy workers too wrapped up in family life behind their shutters to notice our departure.

Chapter 12

Spring Arrives, along with Mike O'Casey

With every day that passes, outdoor life seems to open up before us now. Earlier this month, spring announced her arrival, when we were lured from our dusty *atelier* by the amazing cries of thousands of migrating cranes, as they filled the skies above the presbytery. The noise was deafening and standing in the middle of the garden, gazing skyward, we looked up in awe, at a sight that was just breath-taking.

These huge, long-necked birds with wingspans of up to three feet, created perfect v-shaped formations, as they regrouped above our heads on their migration across France from Spain. Enveloped by the noise, we found ourselves face to face with nature, in a way we had never experienced before, and for the first time, we began to realise, there was going to be so much more to discover in our new life, than we could ever have imagined.

With the arrival of spring and our new-found encounters with nature, we begin to explore the idea of growing our own produce, or creating a *potager*, as the French would say and after reading up on the subject, Ron has spent much of the last two days digging over the chosen area, in preparation for our first planting. Of course being Irish, we are starting with potatoes, mainly because I miss the lovely fluffy ones from home, as opposed the yellowish, rather waxy, potatoes found everywhere in France.

Heading down the garden, the church bell announces midday and time for Ron to hang up his spade for the long ritual of lunch. I think to myself, my rather exhausted-looking husband deserves a bit of a treat. Usually about this time we would share a typically rustic repast under the walnut tree, washed down with a drop of red wine; but today we decide to reward ourselves with a visit to our local restaurant 'La Table'.

Closing the huge door of the presbytery behind us, we step out into the bright, midday sunshine and make our way down the road to our local eatery. Situated on the corner at the end of the street, 'La Table' is a typical, little French restaurant, with its board outside, advertising the *plat du Jour* for ten Euros a head.

To the rear it backs onto *les halles*, a covered area open on all sides, with huge oak beams holding up the roof. *Les halles* would have housed the weekly market in Saint-Allier, until the market at Petit-Villefranche took over. Today it holds a producers market several times a year and is quite a tourist attraction, dating back to medieval times. This lunchtime however, it is set with tables, bedecked in red and white gingham cloths and provides '*La Terrasse*' for outdoor dining.

Pushing the front door open we step into the darkness, until our eyes readjust to the light inside, revealing the bar ahead and several tables scattered around the foyer. Propping up the bar, three local men have commenced the lunchtime ritual and are enjoying a stiff drink before embarking on their four-course meal with wine - an integral part of every French artisans, two-hour lunch break!

Several tables are occupied and as usual silence descends along with our arrival. Most of the locals know who we are, ever since the mayor had us stand up at the '*Salle de Fêtes*', we on the other hand, don't really recognise any of the faces yet. Filling the silence with the obligatory, "*Bonjour Messieurs Dames*," we comply with French etiquette and put the assembled populous at their ease, as they reply in unison, "*Bonjour.*" It is hardly surprising in a small village in rural France like Saint-Allier, that the two foreigners, who bought the old presbytery, are going to be a bit of a novelty for some time to come.

The usual lunchtime noise quickly resumes and we are shown to a table for two in an adjoining room, where several people are already enjoying their meal. We opt for the '*plat du jour*', which consists of a starter of cold meats, terrines, quiches and salad. For the main course there is Veal in a cream sauce with French beans and *pommes-frîtes;* a cheese board follows this and the whole thing is rounded off with a delicious crème brûlé. Included in the ten-Euro price, is a carafe of local red wine.

With our starter carefully selected, we sit back and relax, no longer a novelty; we sip our red wine and slip comfortably into the long French lunch break.

Such a joy it is to swap the physical toil of renovating an old property and turning over the soil, for the sanity of this obligatory hiatus in the day. It is impossible to remember the time pressures of our former lives that rendered Ron so ill; the very physicality of this life is the secret to its health-giving properties. We live in bodies designed to move, I think to myself, not to be tied to a desk, bowed down by pressure, where inside voices warn us to take flight, but the demands of the work place nail us firmly to the spot, adrenalin pumping but never dissipating.

'*Vous êtes terminé*?' The voice of our pretty, young waitress interrupts my thoughts and draws me back into the present. 'Oui, merci, c'était très bon!' I blurt out automatically, as I agree happily to hold back my knife and fork for the next course. Before returning to the kitchen, she looks back over her shoulder and asks, "Have you met Monsieur O'Casey yet? He'll be back in Saint-Allier for the summer this month. You might know him, he's from Ireland and lives at the old cognac farm on the edge of town?"

Taking another sip of wine, we both agree Mike O'Casey is a name we have come across several times, since our arrival in Saint-Allier, but strangely enough, haven't actually bumped into personally back in Ireland. It is a small place we agree, although we have yet to meet all its inhabitants! Our curiosity is aroused however and as we enjoy the rest of our meal, we ponder over whom exactly Monsieur O'Casey is and how he has made such a lasting impression on our fellow villagers.

84

Blinking, we stumble back into the street, with the contented feeling of two people who have dined heartily and make our way in the direction of home. Busily discussing our plans for the rest of the afternoon, we pass the presbytery front door and head down the lane next to the old monastery, to enter by the back gate, as Ronnie wishes to acquaint me with his progress in the *potager*.

Arriving at the gates of the presbytery, we are stopped in our tracks by the sight of Françoise, as she waves enthusiastically and beckons us to join her, in what can only be described as, a rather conspiratorial manner. Talking in a low voice, although we appear to be entirely alone, it is difficult to work out exactly what she is saying at first, but my ears soon pick up the magic words, *apéros* and *Samedi soir*. Hoping Ron has grasped more of this encounter than I have, we bid each other 'au revoir' and retreat to the garden for a debriefing session.

It transpires it is Marie's 80th birthday on Saturday. Marie having been the housekeeper at the presbytery and as it turned out, a jolly good laugh, at our *soiree* earlier in the year. A surprise get-together has been planned in her honour by Françoise, in the form of an '*Apéro Dinatoire*', which is to be held at the old monastery and to include all the neighbours of Saint-Allier Sud, as they collectively refer to themselves. We both feel honoured to be included in this select gathering and set aside an hour before dinner to join them all for a celebratory drink.

During the next couple of days, I help Ron on the *potager*, raising the soil into long runnels, before carefully planting the seed potatoes in neat rows. Standing back to admire our labours, we both agree, it all looks rather professional and giving each other a muddy pat on the back, we make our way over to the old well, with its promise of cool clear water at the drop of a bucket and begin watering them in.

You may be wondering at this point, why we don't simply use a hose, which would of course be a lot less bother. Well, you may have unwittingly just stumbled on the Achilles heel of our agricultural venture. Truth be told, the *potager* is far too far from the house for the hose to stretch and to make matters worse, a hosepipe ban has just been announced by the local *Marie*.

Our first venture into watering the crops is a novelty, however, and as Ron turns the heavy, metal handle, we watch the bucket descend into the murky depths below, waiting for what seems like an age, before hearing the reassuring splash, as it finally hits the water at the bottom. Slowly, Ron winches the heavy, water-filled bucket to the surface and as it appears, I haul it towards me, in the process, somewhat disappointingly, spilling half the contents over myself, before landing it safely on the ground. Looking down into the half-empty bucket, I stand rather forlorn, like a reject from a wet T-shirt contest, thinking to myself, what a lot of effort for so little reward.

Squelchy and wet, I begin the first of many trips to the *potager*, as we repeat the process of hauling bucket loads of water to the surface, sprinkling it over ourselves and more importantly, over our beloved crops. On this first watering session, we are fanned by a gentle breeze and eventually begin to find the whole process therapeutic, as we drift back in time, re-enacting a scene from village life that could have taken place a hundred years earlier.

Finally, heading up the garden to the house, everything having received a thorough soaking, we look back over our shoulders in satisfaction. The last of the sun's rays bathe the *potager* in their golden light and somewhere under the surface new growth is stirring. We hope!

Back in the kitchen, having washed and changed, we are enjoying a pre-dinner drink after our labours, when the doorbell announces a visitor. Murphy predicting an imminent invasion as usual, goes into over-drive, barking like a lunatic and amid the chaos, I am left wondering whom it could be, as we are not expecting guests.

Much to the disappointment of our trusty guard dog, he is bundled unceremoniously into the study, as I open the front door. Blocking the evening light, the frame of a large rugby player fills the doorway and beside him a tall, slim, attractive woman stands. Before I can say anything, like music to my ears, the lilt of the

Dublin accent drowns out the now muffled barking. " A warm Irish welcome to Saint-Allier. My name is Mike O'Casey and this is my good wife, Maeve!"

The bond of kinship wastes no time kicking in, as two Irish families living abroad recognise their shared history and greet each other like long-lost friends. Ushering Mike and Maeve into the sitting room, we are quick to keep the Irish tradition alive and offer our new-found friends a welcoming drink.

Mike a larger-than-life character, with a booming Irish accent has a ready wit. He jovially points out that back home our paths would have been unlightly to cross, but far removed from the troubled land of Ireland, in French fields we embrace our Celtic roots.

Both Ronnie, Mike, Maeve and I, like the majority of Irish citizens, have many friends on both sides of the divide and the fact that two Irish protestants, are now renovating an old catholic presbytery, in South West of France, just gives Mike an Irish catholic, more material than he needs, to have us all in stitches!

As I top up their drinks, Mike explains to us how they stumbled upon the area about ten years earlier, when on holiday with his brother and family. They had fallen in love with the scenery and the people of the area and finding themselves chatting with a local estate agent, while in a bar in Petit Villefranche, were tipped off about an old cognac farm for sale on the edge of the village of Saint-Allier. It needed total renovation but was a handsome example of a wealthy estate, which came with several acres of land and three worker's cottages to renovate.

What follows is a lengthy story and Mike promises to fill us in and give us a guided tour, if we accept his invitation to dinner the following week, to which we readily agree.

Before they leave, we give them a tour of the presbytery. It's a lovely opportunity to share our enthusiasm with a couple that have been along the same path and Mike and Maeve, are very complimentary about our work. They had looked at the presbytery themselves, when it came on the market earlier in the year, just curious to see inside the old building and can't believe the progress we have made in such a short time.

Back in the hallway, we say our goodbyes and agree to meet up again the following week, at the old cognac farm for dinner. Later, as we eat around the kitchen table, we both agree it's lovely to finally put a face to the name Mike O'Casey and have to admit, one can see why the villagers have taken him and Maeve to their hearts. Meanwhile, as our diary fills up with ever more invitations, any fears we might have had of being lonely in our new life are well and truly put to bed.

Speaking of engagements, Saturday night has come around in the blink of an eye and I am just applying a drop of lipstick in preparation for Marie's surprise 80th birthday celebration. In the kitchen, I have left out something simple for the tea and giving each other an admiring glance, we head down the garden arm in arm, through the back gate and along the lane to the old monastery, where we join our neighbours for the surprise '*Apéro Dinatoire*' in honour of the lovely Marie.

Old Jacques, Françoise's husband, greets us at the door and ushers us across an impressive stone entrance hall, through a heavy wooden door, into the enormous kitchen, at the centre of which, is a very long rectangular table and chairs. More wooden chairs line the walls and at the head of the table, a large range cooker takes pride of place.

There appear to be no kitchen units as such, just a huge porcelain sink at the window and a long, heavy, dark-wood dresser laden down with plates, pots and pans and any other kitchen implements one can possibly imagine. No work surfaces as such, but then again, it is obvious, in this kitchen, all the action takes place on the magnificent central table.

Henri and Chantal Buisson, our neighbours, have arrived before us with their little daughter Amèlie and are seated on the wooden chairs around the periphery of the room. Amèlie is pointing excitedly at a huge wide-screen television fixed on the wall to the left of the range. It looks decidedly out of place in this ancient environment, but the French are never too bothered about how things look.

In this case, Jacque and Françoise proudly wax lyrical about the new acquisition, which has brought the joys of French television into their midst. For demonstration purposes only, an inane French game show with its obligatory older male presenter and young female assistant flashes its 60's style frivolity across the screen, in silence.

Chatting to Henri and Chantal, young Jacques Reneau and his wife, Inès, join us and we greet each other in the traditional fashion. By now time is passing and to date no refreshments, in the form of alcoholic beverages have been proffered. This is unfortunate, as my grasp of the French language is much improved, after a drop of the local vino. Meanwhile, around us, the kissing ritual becomes like a free-for-all, making it difficult to remember whom one has kissed and whom one has missed and risked offending.

Finally, an hour after everyone has arrived, silence is called for as the doorbell rings, announcing Marie's arrival. The unsuspecting octogenarian is swiftly ushered into the darkened room, now lit only by the flashing lights of the wide-screen television and is promptly knocked sideways with cries of '*Bon anniversaire*!' as lights go on, revealing 'Saint-Allier-Sud' in all their glory!

Marie revels in the attention and takes the whole thing in her stride, as everyone queues up for more kisses. Drinks are being offered all round and I find myself sipping a chilled glass of *pineau blanc*. It is only later we discover that one of the rules of French etiquette insists the host does not offer any refreshments until all the guests have arrived.

Up to now, our experience of an '*Apéro*' has been a pre-dinner drink with savoury nibbles, lasting about an hour. So you can imagine our confusion, when Françoise begins to usher the assembled throng to allotted seats around the large rectangular table.

Ronnie and I find ourselves seated next to the Mayor, Gilles Charbonnet, and his wife, Danielle on one side and Young Jacques Reneau and his wife Inès on the other. Young Jacques, ever the comedian, playfully ribs Marie across the table and the whole ensemble descends into ripples of laughter, setting the party mood for the evening.

At this point to my surprise, Françoise arrives holding a huge silver platter above her head, which she sets in the middle of the table, revealing an array of glistening oysters, interspersed with wedges of lemon. Cheers go up as they are passed around and silence descends just as quickly as heads go back and the delicious oysters slip down.

No sooner than the oysters have been consumed and the silver platter removed, than plates of piping-hot clear soup are placed in front of each guest and once again everyone tucks in, expressing compliments to Françoise on her culinary expertise.

As bowls are emptied, Old Jacques exhorts everyone to '*Faire Le Chabrol*' and demonstrates the old country tradition, by pouring some of his wine into his soup bowl and lifting the bowl to his mouth, greedily drinks the contents! I can see some of our gathering think this old tradition to be just a step too rustic and coyly decline. Alas, Old Jacques looks over at me with a twinkle in his eye and thinks it most amusing to insist that I give it a go!

Leaping from his chair, he commences by pouring some wine into my soup bowl and to cheers from all assembled, I tilt the large bowl backwards. The next thing I know, the soupy wine mixture is heading my way like a tsunami and rather than slipping down, it splashes my face and I end up wearing more than I manage to consume! Luckily, Old Jacques has anticipated the disaster and is ready with a large napkin to save the day.

Having done my bit to add to the frivolity of the evening, I sit back and enjoy the next course, which is foie gras, glad that the spotlight has finally moved on to someone else! The foie gras is followed by a selection of cheeses and finally around eleven o'clock, the lights are dimmed and an amazing gateau makes its entry, lit by an array of candles.

Just like anywhere else in the world, 'Happy Birthday' is sung and Marie blows out the candles. With her eyes tight closed, she makes a wish and cheers go up again as the lights come back on. Young Jacques is pulling her leg mercilessly about her wish, insisting she was hoping for a '*jeune homme*' to keep her warm when the winter nights return!

Before the end of the evening, Marie is presented with an elaborate bouquet of flowers and everyone parts company - after a final chaotic round of kissing, of course.

Ronnie and I, ambling back through the gates of the old presbytery, discuss how adding the word '*dinatoire*' to an '*apéro*', obviously implies something more than just a pre-dinner drink. It's funny I muse to myself - like the '*apéro dinatoire*'- our new life just keeps on giving.

Chapter Thirteen

The Old Cognac Farm

The road up to the old cognac farm is on the left, just a kilometre outside Saint-Allier and flanked on both sides by a variety of ancient trees. As we bump our way along the lane, looking up, a buzzard hangs motionless in the sky; its beady eyes scan the ground for prey, while below, the rolling hills of the Charente unfold on either side of us, stretching out infinitely. It's a beautiful June evening and at the top of the lane, two cars are parked.

Drawing along side, we find ourselves in what at first glance, looks like a small hamlet. Taking centre stage is the old cognac farm - a testimony to the wealth once created by the production of the rich amber firewater, from which it takes its name. To the right and left of the front door, with its impressive glass fanlight, stretch four windows over two floors, each flanked by pale blue shutters. Two impressive palm trees stand guard at the entrance, giving the whole place a feeling of glamour reminiscent of the French Riviera.

As if on cue, Mike appears round the side of the house; the flamboyant colours of his Hawaiian shirt, mirror the theatrical setting, as his larger than life personality fills the early evening air with his Irish charm.

"So you found us ok! Welcome to 'Belles Côtes' I'll give you a quick tour outside before we go in and meet the others." Ron and I eagerly agree and setting off behind Mike, cross the garden towards a gravel courtyard.

Originally, he tells us, there had been two enormous barns here; one still remains, housing the ride-on mower, amongst other large pieces of mechanical-looking equipment. The second, he explains, has become the stonewall surrounding a large swimming pool; this has been achieved by removing the roof and reducing the height of the walls to shoulder height. Two beautiful wrought-iron gates are fitted where the barn doors would have been and the area around the pool has been stylishly tiled.

Mike points out on the other side of the courtyard, a smartly renovated farmhouse, with holiday accommodation for a family of four. He gives us a quick look inside and we both agree, what he has achieved is really impressive. Our tour takes in two more even bigger farmhouses, all renovated to a similar high standard and providing luxury holiday accommodation in total for sixteen people. The complex is finished off, to the rear of the other two houses, with yet another swimming pool, this time with far-reaching views over the rolling countryside.

Thus, it transpires that this sleepy little hamlet is in fact a fully functioning holiday complex and the pride and joy of its creator. Since the renovation works were finally completed, about ten years ago, Mike and his wife Maeve, have spent every summer here, from May to October, enjoying the long hot French summers and presiding over their own little empire.

Entering the big house by the back door, we find ourselves in a vast kitchen with stonewalls, a high-beamed ceiling and original terracotta floor tiles. At one end a wood-burning stove takes pride of place, surrounded by comfortable armchairs and separating this seating area from the kitchen, a rustic farmhouse table is invitingly set for dinner.

As our eyes take it all in, my attention is drawn to a decadent solid-oak island, where two other guests are seated, enjoying a pre-dinner drink. Maeve, working on the other side of the island, is busy rolling out pastry and everywhere the air is thick with the smell of cooking.

I recognise at once the face of Serge Bertrand the '*maçon*'. He'd done some great work on our roof, shortly after we arrived in Saint-Allier and in fact, possibly saved our lives, after discovering one of the huge chimneys at the presbytery was about to fall in on the bedroom below! He ended up lowering all the chimneys to a less precarious height before completing the other much-needed repairs.

Mike, realising we had met Serge before, introduces Avril his partner, a warm friendly girl with an open, honest smile and a ready wit. The customary three kisses are exchanged, after which one can't help but feel well and truly welcome and as we take our places round the island, we melt effortlessly into the cosy ambiance.

The conversation moves naturally between French and English and as laughter is never far away with Mike around, I pause to admire the relaxed way Maeve prepares the meal in our midst, still managing to contribute to the conversation. It is obvious, as the night goes on and we decamp to the dining table, that Mike and Maeve have made a concerted effort to integrate well into the community and are familiar with local families, the politics of this tiny village and its inevitable scandals.

Having polished off a delicious tomato and goat's cheese tart for starters, Mike insists on cooking the steaks himself and takes the order from each person as to their preference regarding '*cuisson*'. While he is busy showing off his culinary prowess at the cooker, Serge and Avril tell us their story.

It transpires Avril had been widowed in her early thirties and after many years struggling to work and bring up two children alone, had almost given up hope of finding happiness. It was a leaky roof on the eve of her fortieth birthday that unexpectedly set the scene for a handsome young stonemason to enter her life.

At just twenty-two years old, Serge is mature for his age - a serious young man, with a great mop of thick, blond hair. He found himself intrigued by this beautiful, brave and so very capable woman, whose teasing, witty repartee, promised hidden depths that drew him irresistibly towards her, despite the age difference.

In fact while Avril enjoys the evening, filling the room with her fun outlook on life, it's hard to tell which of this happy couple is the elder.

As the night unfolds, Mike proves to be a more than generous host, with an evidently large drinks cabinet. And in typical Irish tradition, keeps everyone's glass topped up, despite protestations that some of us have reached our limit!

It is easy to see how this larger-than-life Irishman, has captured the hearts of the people of Saint-Allier. He has mastered the language, albeit with an endearing Celtic accent and a propensity to throw in the word '*Super Bon*' at every opportunity. Both he and Maeve have gone out of their way to support local village events and have even hosted the annual Saint-Allier day *fête* in the grounds of Belles Côtes.

Ron and I, relaxing, soak up their advice on integrating into French village life along with a smooth glass of Cognac. We are fully clued up on all village scandal and will henceforth look at our rather chubby butcher in a different light, now we know what he's been up to with the postman's wife!

Finally, like all perfect evenings, ours ends with a tour of the hosts vaulted wine cellar. Mike moves knowledgably between the racks, filling us in on the stories behind each acquisition. Famous names such as Nuits Saint George, Margaux, Pomerol and St. Emilion, rest under their dusty covers, maturing quietly, until some suitable family occasion calls upon them to impress the guests with their expensive labels.

Ron and I look on with a tinge of envy. We too have an impressive stone cellar and on a recent trip to St. Emilion, invested in half a dozen bottles of their best red. Placing them carefully on an empty wine rack, I have to say, they did look rather lonely. In fact, they never even got time to collect a respectable covering of dust, before the arrival of unexpected guests one weekend sent Ron scurrying into the cellar to retrieve them. Not one bottle managed to find its way back and so far no more have attempted the intrepid journey down the windy stone steps to our *cave*, where the empty racks wait optimistically.

And so, shortly after midnight, we are released into the balmy evening air, to kiss our friends '*bonne nuit*' and wind our way, rather unsteadily, home. Leaving the car to collect the next day, we amble down the lane. The darkness swallows us up, wrapping itself around us and we find ourselves swaddled in the soft, black velvet of the night. Above us, galaxies of twinkling stars minuscule our existence on this tiny planet and we both agree, had circumstances not forced us out of our comfort zone, we may never have felt so alive!

.

Chapter Fourteen

Kidnapped by the Neighbours!

With windows wide open, the house is filled with the morning sunshine and Ron and I share a coffee around the kitchen table, discussing our hopes to one day, open the old presbytery as a bed and breakfast. The two grand bedrooms at the back of the house facing the park would make wonderful guest rooms. One now boasts a beautiful en-suite and the other sits adjacent to my favourite room of the house, the big family bathroom.

I have had such fun decorating it and choosing the furnishings. After my little three-bedroom semi in Ireland, it's like a dream come true to have such a blank canvas to work on. With its antique fireplace, chaise longue and glass chandelier, I have been inspired by the many beautiful châteaux of the region. Hopefully presenting, on a much smaller scale of course, my own humble homage to their sumptuous grandeur.

I allow myself to think about how great it would be to share our lovely home with guests and for Ron and I, to have the challenge of creating and running our own business when the renovation work no longer takes up all our time. Breaking into my thoughts for a moment, Ron comes up with an idea. "What about a dry run? We could get a couple of friends to act as guinea pigs and book them in for a weekend, pretending to be our first paying guests. It would give us a chance to see if we really are cut out for the role."

"Sounds exciting!" I reply, " And I think I know just the couple for the job - Geoff and Catherine Houston. They were talking about coming over anyway and I'm sure they could be persuaded to sample our hospitality in return for an honest critique of our efforts."

Inside the cosy kitchen, with its pale blue and white tiles and painted walls, we enjoy the break, before contemplating our return to the front bedroom, where yet more wallpapering and painting await our undivided attention. In the background BBC Radio 4 exudes its comforting familiarity, the warm rich tones of the presenters providing an anchor for all those adrift in foreign lands.

Through the open window alas, the sound of birdsong is unsanctimoniously drowned out by the sudden barking of a dog, the chatter of a small child and the enthusiastic tones of Henri, our French neighbour. Murphy announces the imminent invasion, as our tranquil scene is shattered by doorbells and barking animals. Ronnie grabs our poor mutt, as through the window I see Plato take up position at the top of the steps, closely followed by the rest of the Buisson family.

Opening the door, Plato is the first to pile in, eagerly searching out poor Murphy, anxious to show him who's boss again. By now Ron has safely closed the kitchen door, leaving Murphy on the other side to nurse his wounded pride, as Plato struts around the hall, claiming it his own! I do wish Chantal and Henri would leave their dog at home sometimes, but they seem oblivious to the havoc he creates.

In the ensuing chaos, kisses are exchanged and Ron and I attempt not to look totally confused, as we try to work out the reason for this unexpected visit. The only clue would seem to be the repeated mention of the words '*Fromage du Chèvre*'. Now Ron and I enjoy a bit of excitement like the rest of you, but until now goat's cheese hasn't really done it for us. Being typically polite, however, we endeavour to look suitably ecstatic!

"*On doit venir chez nous. Nous allons à la ferme des chèvres*!" Henri announces. Even with my limited understanding of French, I am aware that is not a question but a statement, and that any chance of getting on with our work is now out of the question. Instead, carried along on the euphoria of the moment, we grab our coats and find ourselves heading down the garden towards Henri's car, along with Chantal, Amèlie and the ebullient Plato.

Squashed between Chantal and Amèlie, with Plato hanging over my left shoulder and dribbling uncontrollably, we bump our way up the lane and onto the main highway. In the front I can hear Ron trying to get a handle on exactly where we are going and why.

It seems we are heading into the deep Charentaise countryside with Henri on his fortnightly trip to the goat farm, where he insists the best goat's cheese in France is made. With great enthusiasm he announces we can meet the goats and see where the cheese is made, plus of course '*faire une dégustation*!'

Feeling a bit more clued up now, Ron and I begin to relax. It would have been nice to have a bit of advance warning, but here we are and all we can do is sit back and enjoy the ride.

Eventually, a distinct country aroma indicates the proximity of our destination and we pull into a concrete yard in front of a large barn. Tumbling out of the car we are greeted by a jovial gentleman in clean white overalls and a tidy white hat. He welcomes Henri like a brother, before Ronnie and I are proudly introduced as 'Les Irlandais de Saint-Allier!' Monsieur Bonnet, the farmer, appears dutifully amused that a couple from such foreign parts have made the pilgrimage to his humble goat farm, but is obviously delighted at the opportunity to show off his burgeoning enterprise.

Rather like a small herd of Monsieur Bonnet's own flock, we follow him goat-like into the large barn and find ourselves standing around the perimeter of a huge pen filled with what he describes as his lady goats. The ladies look resplendent in their white coats, with big blue eyes and dainty little pompoms hanging from their chins. Monsieur Bonnet is swollen with pride as he extols the virtues of their milk and the resulting cheese he produces.

The warm heavy air is thick with the sweet, pungent smell of goats' breath and the noise of the ladies bleating is only surpassed by a loud banging coming from the back of the barn. Monsieur bonnet winks in a suggestive manner, "Suivez-moi!" he shouts over the noise and heads off in the direction of the thundering racket.

At the rear of the ladies pen, against the wall are three stalls, from where it appears all the commotion is emanating. As we draw closer our eyes are met by three of the biggest rams I have ever seen. They must be the size of donkeys, with huge horns making them even taller, black coats and rolling blue eyes! Frantically, they kick the doors of their pens in an agitated manner, making us all jump back to a safer distance.

Over the noise Monsieur Bonnet introduces his prize specimens. He goes on to explain how every so often he releases them into the pen, no doubt causing absolute chaos amongst the ladies. For decency's sake at this point, I won't give you the full translation of Monsieur Bonnet's rather graphic description, suffice to say the pride he takes in their performance appears to reflect rather favourably on his own sense of manliness!

Breathing a sigh of relief that the prize rams are not required to perform today, we move on through a door to the right and find ourselves in the heart of the cheese-making process. Our host explains that the huge silver vats take care of pasteurisation and goes on to point out the clean white muslin sacs, where the curds are separated from the whey, before the they go on to be mixed with salt and moulded into appropriately shaped cheeses.

The end of our tour finds us in an office-cum-shop, where Monsieur Bonnet prepares the '*dégustation.*' Several cheeses are spread out on the counter before us and a reverential silence falls upon the proceedings as we each sample his wares. Now, I have always known the French enjoy their food, but since living here I am quite amazed at just how enthusiastic they can become about it. Ron and I manfully join in the chorus of "*Très Bon*!" throwing in a "*Merveilleux*!" and an "*Excellent*!" for good measure.

Finally, the adulation shows signs of abating and I am aware that everyone is waiting for us to make a purchase. Luckily, Ron has some money in his jacket pocket, but there is an anxious moment when we both wonder if we have enough with us. Picking a mild cheese with a pleasant flavour, that will be delicious with a sweet accompaniment of honey and walnuts, we breathe a sigh of relief that we would appear to have 'done the right thing.'

We are not off the hook yet, however, as Henri goes on to suggest we put in a weekly order, which he can pick up for us on his regular visits. Rather taken aback by this unexpected suggestion, as goat's cheese is not necessarily a regular item on our shopping list, we find ourselves agreeing to what would appear to be an unending supply of the stuff!

With our cheeses safely bagged, Henri indicates it's time to head home and we leave a satisfied Monsieur Bonnet with a firm handshake and return to the car. The journey home passes quickly, as we chat easily with Chantal and Henri, while beside me Amèlie continues to look upon me as her best pal, my infantile attempts at her mother tongue putting us both on an equal footing!

Arriving back at the presbytery, the church bell announces the time to be one thirty and waving goodbye to the Buissons, we make our way up the steps to the front door. Back in the kitchen with its blue and white tiles, I stop for a moment and think to myself: Had we just been abducted or was it all a dream? Surely, we were just about to continue decorating the front bedroom?

Chapter Fifteen

A Dry Run for the 'Old Presbytery B&B'

With all arrangements in place, it is only a week now until our guinea pigs, Geoff and Catherine, arrive from Ireland for four nights' bed and breakfast at the currently fictitious 'Old Presbytery *Chambre d'Hôte.*' Preparations are underway for their arrival, although the back bedroom ceiling continues to hang over our heads!

The en-suite in the room is beautiful, but a local builder from the village has been promising to re-plaster the ceiling for what seems like ages. He has finally come up with the morning of the day Geoff and Catherine arrive as his only possible date for a rendezvous and sheer desperation to get the job done has forced me to accept his proposal, knowing full well I might not see him again for months. Mulling the situation over in my mind, I find myself hoping I can have the room cleaned before Ron gets back from Bergerac Airport with our guests.

In the meantime it would seem, word has got out that we are open for business, as a colony of unwanted guests have taken up residence in the '*Potager*'. Ron discovered them yesterday, when he went down to inspect the swathe of green that is our potato patch, or should I say, was our potato patch!

On closer inspection, our guests bear an uncanny resemblance to an old-fashioned sweet called the 'Humbug,' being a creamy colour with brown stripes. That is where the resemblance ends however, as far from being a sweet sugary treat, these little chaps are treating themselves to the fruits of our labours and can't seem to get enough of our free hospitality.

As I speak, Ron is down at the '*potager*' spraying the little blighters with some obnoxious blue substance as recommended by our neighbour Henri. Things are not looking good, however, as on his last report the said beetles, known in France as '*Doryphores*' and more familiarly to ourselves as colorado beetle, seem to look upon the spray as some kind of refreshing shower, letting the cool liquid invigorate them, before recommencing their consumption of our entire crop!

Dirty, tired and worryingly blue in colour from the toxic spray, Ron returns to consult Henri as to what to do next. We had hoped, rather naively perhaps, to grow our vegetables organically, avoiding the chemical pesticides sprayed liberally by our neighbours. According to Henri, however, we are reaping the rewards of our naivety and as he disappears off into his '*dépendance*' chuckling to himself about the folly of '*Les Irlandais*'. He returns a few minutes later with a rusty can marked 'danger.'

Standing in our disappearing potato patch, we look at the can in despair. Who would want to risk eating anything that had survived such an onslaught of toxic chemicals? Reluctantly, we decide to abandon what's left of our beloved crops and leave our hungry humbug guests to enjoy their banquet.

The morning of Geoff and Catherine's arrival dawns still and warm, the clear blue sky promising heat to come. Standing in the kitchen I look down the park to the vegetable patch. One wouldn't be surprised to see a couple of camels pass by, I think to myself, as what was once our *potager* is now more reminiscent of a scene from the 'Gobi Desert'. In fact I would dare to say, there is more life on Mars, than on our vegetable patch!

Thankfully, I don't have long to ponder our horticultural disasters, as the honk of a horn on the other side of the gate announces the arrival of Monsieur Morel, the plasterer and his boy. I should mention at this juncture, it has been an observation of ours, that no self-respecting French artisan ever arrives without his '*Garçon*,' usually a rather shy inarticulate teenager, whose disinterest in the job in hand is only kept in check by his fear of the boss!

Showing Monsieur Morel and his sidekick to the back bedroom, I dare to enquire how long they might be, as I have guests arriving to use the room later that afternoon. Monsieur Morel responds with a sharp intake of breath, obviously a universal expression amongst builders, while '*Le Garçon*' registers nothing. Slipping out of the room quietly, I decide to cross my fingers and hope for the best.

By lunchtime, it is obvious work is underway, mainly due to the tell-tale signs of white plaster dust escaping from the room and leaving a trail from their boots down the stairs and out to the van. On the dot of twelve the church bell rings and the intrepid pair emerge like a couple of ghosts from Dickens' 'A Christmas Carol.' They leave in their van for their two-hour lunch break, no doubt ready for a glass of red to slake their dry dusty throats.

Work recommences at precisely two o'clock and some time later, I wave Ron off on his way to Bergerac. The journey of about an hour and a half should just get him to the airport in time for the arrival at five o'clock of the flight from Dublin.

"Meanwhile, back at the ranch," as they say in the best cowboy films, Monsieur Morel and '*Le Garçon*' are clearing up and reloading their van for departure. I give Monsieur Morel his cheque and wish them both a 'Bonne Soirée.' As they head off down the steps I'm sure I catch, just the glimpse of a smile from the '*Garçon,*' or maybe he was just squinting against the afternoon sunshine?

I, however, am not smiling, as I survey the damage that has to be cleared up before the arrival of our guests. The new ceiling is marvellous, but plaster dust is just about everywhere and not only in the bedroom, it seems to have materialised all over the house!

By five o'clock dust sheets removed, hoovering and dusting complete, I am trying desperately to wash plaster footprints off the wooden floors. Looking at the clock I realise Geoff and Catherine are landing in Bergerac and totally exhausted by my efforts, in what must be twenty eight degree heat, I throw myself prostrate on the bed, gasping like a fish out of water.

Across the landing, the guest bedroom now resembles an oasis of calm and nowhere is there a sign of its earlier chaos. Reluctantly, I drag myself off the bed and into the shower. Just a short time left to transform myself into the perfect hostess!

Ready and waiting, I stretch out on a sunbed in the dappled shade of one of the trees in the garden and reflect briefly on Geoff and Catherine, who I haven't seen for at least two years. We have known each other since our teens and have kept in touch on and off, sharing the various stages of life as they came along.

Catherine is a dear girl, quiet but caring and very practical having reared four children. Geoff on the other hand would be harder to get to know. An active member of the Territorial Army, he is a clever guy with a regimental eye for detail and a military stance. Over the years, however, he has proved himself to be a loyal friend and together they were there for Ronnie and me through the difficult years of his illness, when I have to say, others failed to last the course.

With a few minutes left to myself, I begin to relax and unwind. Looking upwards through the huge branches to the blue sky beyond, tired from my exertions and wrapped in the warmth of the afternoon heat, I find myself slipping into a glorious nap, surrounded by nothing but the sounds of nature.

Creeping into my dreams the noise of a car in the lane drags me slowly back to consciousness. Feeling refreshed and happy after my brief snooze, I run over to open the gates and letting Ron drive in, I wave to Catherine and Geoff as the car pulls up at the foot of the steps.

They emerge blinking into the bright Charentaise sunlight, unaccustomed to the hot dusty smell of a warm country; they look pale beside our now suntanned skin. Without thinking I automatically lean in for the customary three kisses and realise rather too late that Catherine has stiffened like a poker. Unaccustomed to this kind of familiarity, she smiles but takes a wary step backwards, while I wince, as I realise Ron is attempting the same manoeuvre with Geoff.

For one moment, I fear he may well jump back into the car and demand to be returned to the sanity of Belfast, where everyone keeps a wary distance! But pulling himself up to his full military five foot four inches, he manages to regain his composure and just when I think he is about to salute, gives Ron a manly slap on the back and announces, "Good to see you, my old chap!"

Together we take a stroll around the garden, allowing all parties to regain their equilibrium and stretch their legs after what has been a long and tiring journey. The presbytery looks magnificent from the park as we turn around and take in the whole building. The steps leading up to its double-fronted façade, built over huge cellars, require one to look upwards in order to take in the full grandeur of this late eighteenth-century monument to the now declining influence of the Church in France.

Catherine and Geoff look duly impressed at all we have achieved so far and Ron and I are filled with pride as we head back to the house to settle our guests into their new bedroom. Opening the door into the darkness of the hallway, Ron chats happily to Geoff, until through the drone of conversation, I pick up Catherine as she rather timidly exclaims, "Geoff doesn't suffer fools lightly, I am afraid!" Climbing the stairs, I ponder what exactly this could mean and hope quietly to myself that before the end of their stay, neither Ron nor I fall precariously into this unfortunate category!

Slipping into a relaxed familiarity though as the afternoon progresses into evening, we gather in the garden, where Ron has already lit the barbeque and I have set out some salads and crusty bread on our old rectangular table. Catherine and I relax into two comfortable wicker chairs, while Ron offers everyone a glass of wine.

Geoff is busying himself with the barbeque, giving Ron some useful advice on when the coals would be ready to cook the steaks and accepts a glass of red, while Catherine however, explains she has never managed to acquire a taste for alcohol and settles for some sparkling water.

At the given nod from Geoff, Ron puts the first two steaks onto the barbeque, trying valiantly not to feel emasculated by Geoff's intervention into what has always been his private kingdom. Giving them a few minutes on the first side to brown, Ron flips them over for a few minutes on the other side, ready to serve them pink in the middle.

"Do you mind if I take over, Ron, after you've given Heather her's? Its just I'm a bit worried about salmonella. I think it best if I cook Catherine's steak myself." Ron slides a juicy steak onto my plate and reluctantly hands over his cooking utensils with an air of defeat. We then wait for a further, ten or fifteen minutes, while Geoff reduces Catherine's steak to what resembles a piece of shoe leather, before placing it on her plate with a reassuring nod that it is now safe to eat.

In full swing, Geoff throws the last two steaks onto the barbeque and continues to take control of the cooking. Looking over at Ron, I see he is beginning to feel like Murphy after a visit from Plato the dog. Eventually he intervenes to retrieve his own steak, while it is still edible, leaving Geoff to cremate his to his own personal order.

Finally, we all sit around the table in the fading light, Ron and I have long finished our tender juicy steaks, while Catherine and Geoff are still manfully chewing away on their shoe leather, both reluctant to question Geoff's cooking prowess, safe only in the knowledge, they have escaped the dreaded salmonella!

The following morning, Geoff and Catherine announce a comfortable night's sleep in the new guest bedroom, remarking specifically on the cleanliness of the en-suite. It would have been nice to take credit for this myself, but to be honest it has a more to do with the fact that they are the first people to use the facility than my cleaning prowess.

Meanwhile, Ron and I set out our proposed B&B breakfast. While I lay the table and put on the coffee machine, Ron nips out to the *boulangerie* in Petit-Villefranche and returns with a selection of delicious freshly baked *croissants*, *pains aux raisins* and *pains aux chocolats*. Some yoghurt, fresh fruit and cereals, finally complete the spread.

Geoff and Catherine are very sweet and show their appreciation by eating heartily, while giving any suggestions they think might be helpful. It is fun to watch them join in the pretence of our first test drive as they happily play the part of two satisfied customers.

Over the next days, we visit a local pottery in one of France's prettiest villages and have a wonderful daytrip to La Rochelle. Arriving at the thriving seaside port it's such a treat to feel the sea breeze after what has been a really hot week. A wander around the colourful local shops with their post cards and sun hats, interspersed with stylish boutiques, brings us out at the harbour where luxurious yachts sparkle in the early afternoon sun. It's not long before we find ourselves sitting outside one of the numerous seafood restaurants that line the front, sampling *moules frîtes* just metres from the sea. Actually to be more precise, Ron and I sample the *moules frîtes*, while Geoff and Catherine play it safe with steak and chips!

All in all, it has been a great weekend with our old friends and on their last day we stay around the house, where Geoff makes himself useful helping Ron install a fan in our bedroom and Catherine insists on doing a bit of ironing. The afternoon sees the delivery of a long-awaited sofa and chairs for the lounge, which we manoeuvre carefully into position in time for a quiet evening around the television, before our guests head off to the airport in the morning.

The evening proves a relaxing experience for Ron, Catherine and myself, as we sink into the new luxury cream sofa, but alas not so for Geoff. Now, I am not sure if this is the moment where Ron and I may unwittingly have fallen into Geoff's category of "Fools, he doesn't suffer lightly?" As, he is refusing to sit on either the chair or the new sofa, protesting that they are far too light in colour to risk placing his posterior on.

At first we think he's joking and encourage him, saying, "Don't be daft, Geoff, come and sit down and relax!" But Geoff is having none of it and ends up perched on a wooden stool the whole evening, leaving Catherine rather embarrassed and Ron and I feeling like a couple of fools for buying what by implication, would appear to be a totally impractical suite of furniture!

Well, as they say, all good things must come to an end and so it's time to see our old friends off to the airport - probably just in time, as Geoff couldn't have sat on the wooden stool much longer without serious repercussions!   Before leaving the house, they both assure us they have had a wonderful time and would highly recommend the 'Old Presbytery B&B,' as a great place to stay.

Waving them goodbye later that afternoon as they head through security at Bergerac airport, Catherine turns round and blows us a kiss, while Geoff true to form, proffers a brief salute.

Chapter Sixteen

A Little Ex-pat Fun in the Sun

Glad to get the house to our selves again after plasterers and guests have gone, Ron and I settle contentedly into what is a typical week in our sleepy little French village.

Recently, a conversation with Mike O'Casey led to an introduction to Madame Isabelle Dubois, an elegant woman in her late fifties, who lives in a grand house fronting the road at the other end of the village.

Madame Dubois and her husband had spent many years in Hong Kong, where they met Mike, who passes his winters there, dabbling in stocks and shares on the Hong Kong stock exchange. They had been good friends until Isabelle's husband decided to have an affair with a younger woman. At which point she returned to their home in Saint-Allier and has lived there alone for the last six years, presumably awaiting a divorce.

A solitary figure around the village, she prefers to remain in the house and is rarely seen out and about. On the other hand, a regular visitor to Mike's soirées, she cannot be missed in a crowd, as her immaculate dress sense and Parisian poise always guarantee her a second glance.

In Hong Kong, Isabelle occupied herself part-time giving French lessons and it is with this in mind that Mike introduced us, suggesting she might take me on as a pupil.

And so today, I find myself heading down the main street towards Isabelle's house. The church bell in the square announces it is two o'clock and I am on my way for my third French lesson with her.

Passing 'La Table,' the little restaurant on the corner, I notice a large poster for 'Saint-Allier Day' on the twelfth of July and make a mental note to keep the day free in my diary.

Crossing the road to Isabelle's house, I admit to having butterflies in my stomach. Like most French people, although she has a good grasp of English, she is reluctant to use it and insists on conducting everything in French. Reaching up to a rather elaborate doorknocker, I announce my arrival and brace myself for the onslaught.

Isabelle opens the door and walking into the hallway, we greet each other in the traditional manner, as she leads me into her salon. Entering the room, one has the feeling of stepping back in time, finding oneself an integral part of some Renaissance painting. My eyes becoming accustomed to the gloom are greeted with the rich dark hues of red velvet curtains and ancient mahogany furniture, while the jewelled colours of a fruit bowl, caught in the only shaft of light, emphasize the beauty of light and shade. Isabelle herself, immaculately made up, emerges from the background, like a character from the picture and her eyes looking out from the darkness, I think to myself, betray a sadness inside.

"Asseyez-vous, Madame," she suggests politely, beckoning me to take my place at the huge dark mahogany table, where an exercise book rests, open at the page where we left off. Without further ado, she launches into a stream of fast-moving fluent French.

Manfully I keep up, learning quickly, as she helps me with pronunciation, which she explains, is the key to being understood. As a French woman, she knows the pitfalls English speakers fall into when arriving in France and explains how we use the word 'bon' or 'bonne' much too often and in the wrong context. We should instead be using 'bien,' things are 'Très bien.' 'Très Bon,' being more appropriate for describing objects like food and drink.

Giving Isabelle my full attention, the first half hour passes quickly, until gradually I find myself beginning to flag. My concentration follows the shaft of light out the window and into the street beyond, where the Church bell announces the half hour. Madame

111

Dubois is in the process of explaining some important grammatical point, which I fail to understand on her first explanation.

She tries again, but still to no avail. If only she would give in and offer a quick clue in English, I think to myself, but that would be against the rules. Stubbornly she persists, unaware that by now, she might as well be trying to explain 'the off side rule' to a member of the Women's Institute! My brain getting more and more confused by the minute, I cannot understand the explanation, never mind the grammatical point!

With a withering look, she decides to put the exercise book to one side in favour of a bit of French conversation. Gradually, my concentration returns via the shaft of sunlight, back into the room, as like two women anywhere, we slip naturally into a deep discussion around village affairs.

Released back into the sunlight half an hour later, I return to the presbytery. Oddly, I have to make a conscious effort to revert back to English, when I find Ronnie washing some paintbrushes in the old porcelain sink in the kitchen. He smiles, delighted to see my improvement. Secretly, he looks forward to the day, when he can take a back seat and we share the responsibility of dealing with French bureaucracy.

Going our separate ways again, Ron heads out to the garden and into the shed, where he releases 'La Bête,' as Henri refers to our enormous petrol-driven mower and prepares to cut the grass. Inside, donning my old clothes, I return to the front bedroom and continue glossing the skirting boards, a job which is beginning to feel more like painting the forth river bridge!

Recently, once a month, Thursday mornings have presented me with a new challenge, my first real foray into the expat community. Up until now I have made a conscious effort to integrate into French village life and this has been really successful. I haven't felt the need to look outside our little hamlet, but it was inevitable that soon the expat community would find me!

112

Becoming friendly with a girl named Joanne Sloan and her partner Dave Mortimer from the French language class, on a Tuesday evening, turned out to be the origin of my first invitation to the book club,' which meets once a month at '*La Ferronnerie*' in Petit-Villefranche.

The group call themselves 'The Book Club' but as it turns out, this term is applied loosely, as books themselves play a very small part in the proceedings. Events centre mainly around freshly baked cakes and a lot of chat. Secretly I have to admit I really enjoyed the last meeting. I say this rather reluctantly, integration being our first priority, but as this side of things is well underway, I think I can allow myself the guilty pleasure, of a good chinwag in my mother tongue.

Thursday morning dawns promisingly bright and throwing my old painting clothes to one side, I dive into the wardrobe. Searching for something light and summery to wear, I make the most of this opportunity to get dressed up and decide on a floral sundress, instead of my paint-splattered jeans.

Ready to go I head out to the car, passing Ronnie in the hallway. Looking up from what he's doing, a cheeky wink acknowledges his approval and as I skip down the steps and into the car, I feel my confidence grow as I begin to make friends, head out on my own and carve a place for myself in this new country.

'*La Ferronnerie*' used to be the old ironmongers in Petit-Villefranche. A place where the intricate wrought iron gates and railings, on display all over the region, would have been crafted by skilled artisans. Originally the site comprised the master craftsman's house, a rather grand double-fronted affair and several workers' cottages, barns and workshops. Its position down a private lane, just off the town's main square, affords it total privacy, with all the advantages of this pretty market town on its doorstep.

When Val and Jonathan Brown, who now own '*La Ferronnerie*', originally found the place, its days as an ironworks were already in the distant past and for some time, the big house and adjacent buildings had been converted into a bed and breakfast, with four gîtes and a swimming pool. The whole complex however, had been renovated in the early sixties and now rather tired looking, was just waiting for a couple with fresh vision and enthusiasm to take advantage of its amazing position.

Just five minutes from the presbytery, I arrive in Petit-Villefranche and entering the square, take a sharp turn to my left, down a lane sign posted 'La Ferronnerie.' At the bottom of the lane, past three of the gîtes, a massive weeping willow frames the garden of the main house. A pretty terrace is set with a table and umbrella against the strengthening sun and chairs are placed randomly, some spilling over onto the grass. Beneath the willow tree, a golden labrador sleeps oblivious to the world.

There are two vehicles parked to the side of the house and the gentle drone of conversation coming from within tells me I am not the first to arrive. Abandoning my car alongside the others, I head indoors in the direction of the voices.

The hallway is welcoming and homely, with the paraphernalia of family life strewn everywhere and in the bright sunlight from the open door, dust dances merrily in the half-light. Glancing through to the room on my left, in search of Val and the others, I discover a large sitting room. Old squashy sofas strewn with brightly coloured throws are arranged around a massive stone fireplace, housing a wood-burning stove and everywhere the walls groan under the weight of hundreds of books.

I take the door to my right and call out, "Hello, anyone home?" Entering the room, a huge oak table predominates, obscuring yet another stone fireplace and wood-burning stove. Through a door at the back of the room, I hear Val shout, "Come on through! We're in the kitchen."

My nose has by now homed in on the smell of baking and I follow both the voice and the delicious aroma into a sun-filled kitchen. Val has a pinny on and with the aid of a pair of oven gloves, is removing a batch of freshly baked scones from the oven. Jonathan her husband, my friend Joanne from the language class and

114

another girl I don't yet know, come forward to welcome me with the usual kisses, everyone happy to embrace the customs of our adopted country.

Val introduces me to Maggie, a friend of Joanne's. Maggie is in her late forties, small but with a friendly outgoing personality and as I am later to discover, has a genuine interest in reading, in fact she is a bit of a bookworm. Whether she has always been that way is hard to tell. Joanne insists her husband, Guy, twenty years her senior, seems to have more interest these days in doing up old vintage cars, apparently spending most of his time in the *dépendance* with Gertrude, his classic Ford.

Maggie and I strike up an immediate friendship and, as the others start to arrive, we all head out to the terrace, everyone eager to get a seat under the parasol, safe from the mid-morning sun. Val's arrival with the scones closely followed by Jonathan, with a large pot of coffee, catches the attention, of what is now a group of about fifteen ladies.

You could say this is the type of coffee morning one would find anywhere in the British Isles, in that we are a group of women enjoying coffee and scones together and you would be right; but there are elements of "The Book Club" that are unique to our situation and make it a valuable part of life abroad.

The conversation here is not idle gossip, but is about swapping information on how to keep warm in the winter, about wood infestation and termites. It is about easing the loneliness of being separated from family and friends and of course, the comfort of being able to communicate in one's mother tongue.

It is fascinating to hear the stories behind the faces as coffees are topped up and the plate of scones reduced to a pile of crumbs. It soon becomes apparent that so many people come to France having made the decision after some life-changing event. When I think of it, lots of people dream of moving to France, but at the end of the day, its quite a brave step to actually up sticks and do it and that is why in many cases, it is those pushed to the edge, that finally have the courage to jump.

And what a happy bunch of people they are now. People like Wendy and Harold Gibson, whom I mentioned earlier, are members of the language class. Wendy recognises us in the sea of faces and joins Maggie and me in the shade of the parasol.

"How's Harold?" I enquire, as I know he is suffering from Parkinson's disease. "Oh he's doing well, his current medication is keeping him stable and we are enjoying life one day at a time." Wendy is an artist in her mid-sixties and has her own health issues, suffering from a respiratory problem, which has meant taking steroids for many years, but she never complains. A pretty, delicate, blonde lady, she dresses colourfully, her clothing giving a subtle nod to her hippy past and a gentle clue to her arty personality.

Full of fun, she smiles as she relates Harold's hobby of collecting war memorabilia ever since his discharge from the army due to ill health. Her love for him is obvious, as she quite cheerfully describes how one room in their home has been given over entirely to his collection of medals, defused grenades and war paraphernalia! Maggie looks on knowingly, but without the same loving feeling, as she reflects on the *dépendance*, where her elderly husband Guy, gets up close and personal with Gertrude the classic Ford!

As people prepare to leave, Maggie says her goodbyes and slips off to the dusty sitting room to browse the bookshelves, in search of another story in which to lose herself and as I locate my handbag, Wendy enquires if Ron and I would like to join them for supper, on Saturday night.

Happily accepting her invitation and scribbling down some directions, I take my leave and head off down the lane past the gîtes. On the short journey home, I can't help reflecting as I look out across the fields: "Coffee and scones with friends on a sun-drenched terrace has got to be the icing on the cake of my new adventure!"

On Saturday night, Wendy's directions lead us over the hill to a cluster of houses at the top of the next valley and following the wooden signs marked 'Chez Gibson' we arrive at the end of a long, winding track. In front of us a small but perfectly formed farmhouse perches at the top of the valley, its cream walls punctuated by delicate green shutters framing French windows overlooking the view beyond.

As we step out of the car into the balmy, early evening air, all is silent apart from the crickets hiding in the long grass. Below the farmhouse, a small terrace is carved into the hillside and a simple table is set for supper.

Wendy appears from the side of the house, clutching a great bunch of lavender from her garden and we share our three kisses engulfed by its delicate perfume. "They're for you," she insists, "come and meet Harold and I will wrap them in some paper." Ron and I follow her into the half-light of the kitchen and are met by Harold hurrying from the back of the house, eager to make our acquaintance.

"Bonjour!" he announces in a broad Lancashire accent, " Lovely to meet the pair of you, Wendy has been telling me all about you." Harold is a thin, grey-haired man, slightly stooped and a little unsteady on his feet due to his illness, but one is drawn to the smile on his kind, honest face. Looking into his eyes, it is impossible not to notice the mischievous twinkle of a man still full of enthusiasm for life.

Together, they show us around the house they bought some twenty years earlier, after Harold had been retired from the army. Their pot of money would have been meagre and the house when they bought it was almost a wreck. Slowly and painstakingly they did a lot of work themselves, Wendy often bearing the brunt of it through cold winters' days when icy winds blew across the valley as they worked hard to make their home warm and secure.

Their labours finished several years ago now and they enjoy life in this beautiful place, their little farmhouse full of Wendy's artwork and of course, Harold's war collection.

Retiring to the garden, we take our places at the table, where it sits into the hillside, commanding breathtaking views across the valley. It's hard to believe that Wendy and Harold, with their tiny pot of cash, have managed to procure for themselves, one of the most beautiful settings I have ever seen. A breath of air gently wafts the tablecloth as Wendy pours us a glass of chilled rosé and looking up, Harold emerges from the house, wearing a German Storm Trooper's helmet!

And so the scene is set. As we learn to understand Harold's eccentricities, he entertains us with his war stories, making no mention of his bizarre headgear! Wendy, used to his slightly unorthodox ways, just smiles and chats away about her life as a painter in the Spode potteries, where she decorated plates to bring in an income during the early years of their marriage.

As we laugh our way though three delicious courses, dusk falls over the valley and only candles and the stars overhead illuminate our little table, revealing Harold's new headgear for each course. Eventually, the cheese arrives served by our host, now sporting a leather flying helmet as last modelled by Douglas Bader in some fading photograph of the Second World War.

Finally, we take our leave at the end of a fun-filled, if not slightly bizarre, evening. Looking back at the old farmhouse as we climb into the car, I can just make out Wendy waving by the light of the moon and next to her, the silhouette of a chap from the First World War trenches, wearing a tin helmet and khaki overcoat, calling out, "*A bientôt*" in a Lancashire accent!

Chapter Seventeen

Saint-Allier Day

The twelfth of July, to anyone originating from Northern Ireland, has always been a significant date. To some, it is a day to celebrate the Protestant tradition, while to members of the Catholic community, often a day more to be endured than enjoyed. For the remaining population, it can be an inconvenience, when parades make it hard to get around and more often than not, on occasions, there can be trouble on the streets.

Ron and I have grown up in this divided society and it has not gone unnoticed that this year the twelfth of July just happens to be the date our adopted village has chosen to celebrate Saint-Allier Day!

So, freed from the restrictions of our past life, Ron and I can't wait to see how our little village intends to celebrate its special day. Instructed by the poster outside 'La Table,' we are wearing walking shoes and equipped with a bottle of water. Murphy follows obediently at our side as we close the presbytery door and head for the rendezvous point in front of the '*Salle des fêtes*.'

Turning the corner and proceeding up the hill, we can see a crowd gathering in the car park opposite and as we get closer, more and more people appear from every direction, giving the impression some giant magnet is drawing the whole village together.

In the bright morning sunlight, the colourful scene is accompanied by cries of "*Bonjour*" and "*Ça va?*" as everyone prepares to share in the planned festivities. Over in the corner of the car park, a donkey makes his presence known by braying loudly, determined not to be left out of the proceedings.

Familiar faces emerge from the crowd everywhere. Mike and Maeve O'Casey, glad to see we have taken their advice about supporting village events, call us to join them as the mayor takes centre stage and raising a loudhailer to his mouth announces, "*Bienvenu tout le monde, au Jour de Saint-Allier!*"

A loud cheer goes up from the crowd and the donkey brays in agreement, as *Monsieur le Maire* begins his speech. With great enthusiasm, he relates the day's itinerary and as we all listen intently, I notice behind him, little Amèlie is waving at me from where she stands beside Henri and Chantal.

The Mayor outlines the day ahead. We are to start from the car park, on what will be a two-hour '*randonnée*' taking us across fields and up onto a plateau of land on the edge of Mike O'Casey's cognac farm, which drops away giving a wonderful vista across the countryside.

Mike has already told us about this beautiful place and we have had some wonderful walks there with Murphy. Ron and I have christened it the 'Edge of the World', because when you stand and look down from the plateau, that is just the feeling one gets!

The walk will continue across rolling countryside, stopping off at "Chez Rousseau," the home of a wealthy surgeon from Paris, where we will enjoy refreshments and a talk from Monsieur Rousseau himself on the history of the region and its architecture.

Following our stop off, we will continue to walk until returning to Saint-Allier, we gather at '*Les Halles*' behind '*La Table*' for "*Une Casse-Croûte*" or picnic lunch.

In the afternoon, there is to be a recital of classical music in the church, after which proceedings will resume again at seven o'clock in the evening, when we are to return to '*Les Halles*' for a sit-down meal, followed by dancing until the early hours.

His resumé complete, it is just left to the mayor to announce that, "Any elderly or infirm villagers are welcome to hop aboard the donkey and cart, which has been laid on for their convenience" and with a final, *"Bonne Chance,"* he wishes us all good luck as we set off accompanied by the braying donkey and its elderly cargo.

What an amazing sight we must make, almost a hundred people closely followed by a donkey and cart, leaving the '*Salle des Fêtes'* behind and heading off across the fields. Ron and I keep a look out for Murphy in case he gets lost in the crowd and I breathe a sigh of relief as Henri and Chantal join our group, this time minus the bold Plato!

Making our way along the edge of the fields towards the plateau, the person beside us regularly changes as everyone sets a different pace and we find ourselves in conversation with people from the village we have never met before.

To the right and left of us, fields of sunflowers taller than us both turn their yellow heads towards the sun and as we look down from the plateau to the 'Edge of the World,' Ronnie squeezes my hand, neither of us able to believe how far we have come from our previous lives.

Continuing on our way, we pace ourselves by the crosses set out at equal distances at the roadside as we wend our way along a route, not far from the original Pilgrim's way to St Jacques de Compostelle, taken by the monks of old on their pilgrimage to Spain.

Eventually, good news from the front announces that 'Chez Rousseau' is in sight and a great cheer spreads along the line, until it reaches the donkey at the back, who, never one to be left out, is unable to resist throwing his head up and joining in.

'Chez Rousseau' is situated at the top of the valley and surrounded by trees. Following the others, we take the long driveway up to the house and find ourselves in the shady garden of an old Charentaise farmhouse and its stone-built outhouses.

Trestle tables bedecked in clean, white linen cloths are set out under the trees, weighed down by jugs of iced water, orange juice and carafes of local red wine. Very soon the garden is host to the

121

whole village, as we enjoy a cool drink and relax in the shade of the trees.

Chatting and walking around the garden, we stop to appreciate the amazing views across the valley and feeling revived, are treated to a fascinating talk and slide show in the barn by Monsieur Rousseau, who shares with us his passion for local history and architecture.

Heading off back down the driveway towards Saint-Allier, I mull over the thought that, never before have I been on a walk which exercised not only the body but also the mind. My daydreams are filled with the history all around me, as I leave the country roads behind and heading back towards the village, take my place at one of the long tables with its red and white checked cloth set out for lunch under '*Les Halles'*.

Despite the energy expended on our walk, lunch is a noisy affair. Ron and I are seated at a table alongside our neighbours, Henri and Chantal, our old friends Marie and Pierre Junot, plus several people from the French language class and of course Mike and Maeve O'Casey.

Our *déjeuner* of soup, crusty bread, cheeses and pâté is well washed down by copious amounts of red wine and Mike has just ordered cognac for everyone when the mayor gets up to introduce Monsieur Lambert from the water board, who is to be our lunchtime speaker.

Puzzled glances convey a certain amount of scepticism as to the entertainment value of our speaker, as Monsieur Lambert takes to the microphone. "*Bonjour Messieurs Dames*," he commences with confidence, as he launches into a lecture on the merits of our local plumbing and sewerage!

His audience, by now slightly the worse for wear having downed the Cognac, appear restless and a ripple of laughter from Mike's direction, finally evokes a reprimand from Monsieur Le Maire!

Our attention returns to the speaker in time to hear him impress on us the excellent quality of tap water in the village. He is obviously rather frustrated at the number of villagers who would rather cart home huge plastic containers of bottled water from the supermarket, than avail themselves of the luxury commodity, he assures us, is pouring out of our *robinets*!

Finally, reassured that all our plumbing needs are being totally catered for, Ron and I share hugs and kisses with our fellow villagers and as the mid-day sun reaches its hottest, head home for a well-deserved siesta.

Tired after our long walk and the added pressure of speaking French at the same time, we take a break from proceedings and spend the afternoon on a sun bed under a tree in the garden, before heading indoors to shower and get dressed for our *soirée* in '*Les Halles*' at seven o'clock.

Resplendent in our evening clothes and ready for a night out, we make our way down the deserted main street. The still evening air is broken by the sound of the church bell as it chimes seven o'clock and from behind 'La Table', music drifts around the corner.

Arriving at '*Les Halles*' things are underway. Tables have been moved and placed around a dance floor; a DJ busies himself, making sure the music keeps coming. To one side in the open air, a hog is rotated on a spit, the smoke rising upwards, an indication to the lack of any movement in the night air and from the great wooden beams, coloured fairy lights illuminate the proceedings.

Unsure where to put ourselves at first, Ron and I take a seat at one of the tables and thankfully, it isn't long before Pierre Junot appears through the steadily growing crowd. He offers to get us both a pineau from the bar and suggests we join them at their table. Pierre and Marie take us under their wing, allowing Ron and I to relax, knowing they will keep us right as the evening unravels. People are arriving by the minute now and Marie explains that Saint-Allier's soirées are famous all over the area, people buying tickets from many of the neighbouring towns and villages.

Through the crowd friendly faces appear and disappear. Henri and Chantal join us with Amèlie, who like many of the children in the village, is allowed to stay up for the occasion and Mike and Maeve

O'Casey tag on at the end of the table as plates of the delicious hog roast are passed down the line.

The music plays and as the meal progresses, a different wine is served with each course. The final course of *Tarte Tatin* arrives accompanied by a sweet dessert wine and as all is finally polished off and the minds of our fellow revellers turn to dancing.

Glancing towards the night sky through the open, upright beams of '*Les Halles*,' stars fill the firmament and as the music plays on, Ron asks me to dance. Joining a sea of smiling faces on the dance floor, we take our place amongst the revellers, while around us the sleepy, silent streets of Saint-Allier lie empty as the villagers party the night away.

It's about two in the morning when we eventually slide into bed in the presbytery and as we drift off to sleep, the sounds of Saint-Allier Day still waft upwards from the village, dancing quietly around the bedroom walls as we fall into a deep and contented sleep.

Chapter Eighteen

United in Grief, Our Voices Become One

Village life gets back to normal after the celebrations and as we do each morning, Ron and I wash and prepare for the day in our beautiful salle des bains. The windows open to the village street below, allowing the sound of Françoise's cries of "*Bonjour*!" to echo through the casement as she greets the boulanger and collects her baguettes for the day.

Noticing we are open to the world, she doesn't miss the opportunity for a bit of gentle ribbing, and calls up from the street below, "*Les irlandais, ils dorment bien, oui*?" Ron and I just look at each other and smile. The fact that we get up around eight in the morning is a cause of great amusement to our neighbours, who have all their work done by the time we commence our ablutions. Ron, his face still covered in shaving foam, heads in the direction of the window and leaning over, calls out, "*Bonjour Françoise*! *Ça va*?" And so begins another day in village life.

Living in Saint-Allier, like everywhere else, has its ups and downs. The sun doesn't always shine and renovation work can sometimes be an uphill struggle in a hot climate, but Ron and I have found our niche in this tiny community and when sadness knocks on their door, it knocks on ours too.

And so, later in the afternoon around five o'clock, when I answer a knock on the presbytery door, I am met by the distraught figure of our neighbour, Françoise. Ushering her gently into the hallway, I realise there are tears in her eyes and through her tears, I can just make out the words, " C'est Jacques Reneau, il est mort!"

Looking into her elderly face, lined by years of working in her potager under the relentless hot sun, I search for an explanation. "Not young Jacques!" I exclaim. "He's only in his early forties!" "C'est pas possible?"

Ronnie joins us from the garden and I am grateful for his help as we try desperately to translate. Françoise pours out the news of how our funny, lovable friend, always the joker and life and soul of our *soirées*, had lost his life on his way home from work, on the road from Angoulême to Saint-Allier.

He had been riding his moped and become stuck behind a large lorry, unable to see the road ahead and eager to get home, he had taken a risk and pulling out around the lorry, was unaware of a fast car coming towards him on the opposite side of the road. He didn't stand a chance.

Huddled in our little group in the hallway, we share our grief, saddened at our loss and yet so privileged to be there to support our elderly neighbour.

Over the next days, as Saint-Allier Sud comes to terms with its loss, the local papers relate the story, printing details of the funeral to be held in the suburbs of Angoulême at Jacques' family Church on Wednesday afternoon.

Talking to Henri and Chantal, we learn Jacque's' widow, Inès, is devastated. Jacques has two children from an earlier marriage, but he and Inès have only been married three years and had plans to start their own family in the near future. Their love was still young and full of promise - he was Inès' first husband and her life. The day of the funeral arrives and as arranged with Henri and Chantal, we join them in their car for the journey to Angoulême. Driving out of our lane, Young Jacques' house on our left lies empty, the shutters closed to the world. On the other side of the lane, the house of his dear friend and neighbour, Old Jacques, reflects its silent image. The whole of Saint-Allier Sud lies empty as the cortège of cars leave the village for the funeral in Angoulême.

The atmosphere in Henri's car is subdued and it gives me the opportunity to look out the window. The road to Angoulême passes through rolling fields of sunflowers, stretching out on either side of the car their vastness only surpassed by the enormous expanse of blue sky, dotted with fluffy white clouds. As we approach the city, our eyes are drawn up to where it sits perched on its rocky promontory, safe within its fortified ramparts. We skirt the centre of the city this time and head for the suburbs where Jacques grew up and where his family church awaits the arrival of those who knew and loved him.

Henri pulls into the crowded car park by the church and carefully avoids the large number of people milling around as they make their way inside. He has difficulty finding a parking space at first, but finally tucks the car into a narrow space next to the wall. Getting out, we begin to have some idea of just how popular Jacques was, as we are swallowed up in the crowd and somehow miraculously emerge next to our mayor, Gilles Charbonnet and his wife, Danielle. It is not long before the rest of Saint-Allier Sud join us and we enter the church as one.

Inside it is filling up fast, but we manage to find three rows together and settling into our seats, Françoise sits to my left with her husband, Old Jacques, while Ronnie is to my right, next to Gilles and Danielle. Behind us, Henri and Chantal sit with little Amèlie, at the end of the row. Looking around, I notice Chantal comforting Marie, who cannot believe Young Jacques will never make her laugh again.

As our eyes adjust to the sombre light inside, I can just pick out the figure of Inès, as I look through the crowd to the front of the church. She sits at the end of a pew, her left shoulder almost touching the coffin of the man she loves.

In different places around the walls, there are pictures of Jacques looking young and handsome, dressed smartly in a white shirt and tuxedo. In the background, the sound of a tenor's voice floats over the hum of conversation as people take their seats.

Françoise leans towards me, "Can you hear the tenor's voice?" she enquires. "Yes, it is very beautiful!" I reply. "It is a recording of young Jacques. He was quite a famous singer you know and made many records."

Ron and I look at each other. How come we didn't know this about our good friend and neighbour? To us he was just Young Jacques, the incorrigible joker with a twinkle in his eye, but to all these people gathered, both inside and outside the church today, this is Jacques, the amazing tenor, who taught music in the college at Angoulême. Did this talented, modest man never talk of his career? Or perhaps somehow, it is quite possible, we missed the fact, lost somewhere in translation?

As proceedings begin, we find ourselves swept along amidst the congregation, shoulder-to-shoulder with our French neighbours. Halfway through the service, we follow Old Jacques out of the pew and form a queue in the centre isle. Passing the coffin we each take a silver spoon, and copying those ahead of us, Ron and I take some holy water and sprinkle it over the coffin. At this point each person passes Inès and pays their respects. As I wait my turn in the queue, for one moment, I can't think of the French words to say and then it comes to me and as I bend down to kiss Inès on the cheek, I offer "*Mes Condoléances!*"

Back in our seat as we bow our heads, the priest announces, 'The Lord's Prayer.' Beside me I hear Françoise begin, "*Notre Père auquel l'art dans le Ciel.*" Realising I don't know the French, I join her in English, "Our Father which art in Heaven" and as we continue our voices become one, the two languages melting together and uniting us in our grief. If ever there is to be a defining moment, when I feel truly accepted in my new life, this will always stay in my mind, as that moment.

Leaving the Church and stepping out into the light, the car park is filled with the sound of Jacques' voice, singing in the beautiful French language of love. We say our goodbyes to each other and climb into the car, as we begin the drive home, taking the same route, that only days earlier, had claimed the life of our dear friend.

The following day is to reveal one final twist in this sad episode of village life. As it turns out, the people of Saint-Allier were not the only ones to read the local papers. Anyone in France will be aware that the death of someone like Jacques means the whole village will attend his funeral and it would therefore be easy to predict, that the area around Jacques' home would be deserted.

And so it was, that as we buried our dear friend, burglars ransacked Jacques' empty house, taking whatever they could.

Chapter Nineteen

Bonjour Darling

It is rare in village life, that a knock on the door brings such bad news. Normally it's one of the neighbours bearing gifts from their potager, as they share the abundance of their crops; and so, as village life gets back to normal, we support Inès in the weeks ahead. On Friday morning the Boulanger opens again and the sound of village life returns to the streets below our Salle des Bains.

Being Friday, we prepare for our usual trip to the Intermarché at Petit Villefranche, to stock up on provisions for the forth-coming week. Descending the steps, closely followed by Murphy, I notice the air is fresh and the heat tempered, due to a huge thunderstorm during the night and so, taking pity on my furry friend, who is always ready for an adventure, I pick Murphy up and pop him in the boot of the car.

Over the last months, we have found the weather to follow a predictable pattern. After a thunderstorm, for a day or so, we enjoy warm sunny weather, then gradually the temperature builds getting hotter by the day, until eventually it reaches the high thirties, when we experience a dramatic thunderstorm that clears the air, allowing the cycle to begin again.

Arriving at the Intermarché and inserting my one euro in the slot, to release a trolley, we set off inside, leaving Murphy parked under the shade of a nearby tree, with the windows down. Shopping can be a bit of a challenge at first, when one arrives in France. There is, as you would imagine, an abundance of fresh

130

fruit, vegetables and herbs to inspire one. Not all regimental in size, as in supermarkets back home I must point out and I often find myself chuckling, when I come across some definite contenders for Esther Rantzen's 'naughty vegetable of the week!'

There is also a lot less ready prepared food; resulting, as I have mentioned before in my forced return to the art of 'haute cuisine.' With culinary exploits in mind, stopping at the cheese counter is a delight, it being possible to spend half the morning there, chatting and sampling cheeses from all over France! The only other thing to mention would be, similar to the market, it is common to find horsemeat on the butcher's counter and a tank of live crabs and lobsters, awaiting their fate at the fish stand!

So when I finally emerge with my trolley full of food and wine, I leave Ron to load up the boot and putting Murphy on his lead, take him for a well-deserved jaunt around the car park to stretch his legs.

This particular Friday, as we circumnavigate the said car park, in search of a blade of grass, meeting Murphy's exacting standards, I am pulled up in my tracks, by a woman's voice of operatic proportions, calling out "Bonjour Darling!" Turning around, my gaze is met by a middle-aged lady dressed in flamboyant colours, with masses of curly grey hair. As she approaches, rather like a galleon in full sail, I notice she is being propelled along in the wake of two Shih Tzus' keen to introduce themselves to Murphy.

As the dogs get on with their usual ritual of introduction, involving a lot of sniffing around various parts of their anatomy, the humans take the more civilised route and my new friend introduces herself, in a rather stumbling 'Home Counties' version of French "Je m'appelle Joyce, darling. Vous avez un chien aussi!" I quickly relieve her of the need to pursue the conversation in a foreign language, saying, "Yes, his name is Murphy" and she breathes an obvious sigh of relief.

There follows a stream of conversation from Joyce, liberally punctuated by the word 'Darling,' during which time, it is impossible to get a word in edgeways! Needless to say, within a few minutes, I practically know her whole life story; how they arrived in France just six months earlier and were still finding their bearings. Like most foreigners one meets, they are in the throws of a renovation project and have just emerged from the 'BricoMarché', our local DIY store, with a boot full of insulation.

Joyce points out her husband, Gerry, where their car is parked in front of the store, as he wrestles the last bale of 'laine de verre' into the back of their four wheel drive. Gerry looks about six foot three tall, with a thick beard and is wearing some rather long shorts and sandals, with a pair of pristine white socks. Realising his gregarious wife has yet again struck up friendship with a complete stranger, he obligingly acknowledges Murphy and me, with a friendly wave.

It begins to dawn on me, Ronnie is probably getting bored by now in the car and Murphy is keen to shake off the somewhat over enthusiastic advances of Sybil and Thorndyke (Thorny for short), Joyce's two 'Shih Tzus'. Thus turning to go, I find myself caught off guard, as Joyce reaches out and grabs me by the arm, " But darling, you and Ronnie must call in for drinks! Shall we say Sunday evening around five o'clock? It would be such fun!"

Suddenly time stands still, as my mind searches in vain for an excuse and although inside my head I can hear Ron's voice say, "You agreed to what?" I find my mouth opening and as if from nowhere, hear myself utter the words, "That would be lovely Joyce. Such fun! See you on Sunday then."

And so, here I am, sitting in the 'Old bread oven' at Joyce and Gerry's, clutching a chilled glass of Rosé, accompanied by a rather grumpy husband, still complaining that he has had enough socialising to do him a lifetime.

For all her talk, Joyce turns out to be an enthusiastic hostess and a guided tour of her 'Longère,' reveals she has an eclectic taste in antiques and a talent for interior design. Her style is of course, very 'Country Homes Magazine' and what she has created, is in fact, a little corner of England in the heart of rural France.

Our tour finishes in the old bread oven, which has been carefully renovated by Gerry to create a shady arbour. Furnished with faded wicker chairs, festooned in arts and crafts cushions and hand made soft furnishings, it nestles in what can only be described, as the most beautiful English cottage garden I have ever seen. Around us basking in the evening sunshine, the garden is alive with butterflies, exotic moths and hungry bumble bees laden with pollen.

The setting is so beautiful, in fact, that even Ronnie mellows after a glass or two of wine and as we chat to our hosts, we find they have a sense of humour not unlike our own. We share our stories in this tranquil setting, surrounded by the scent of the garden and learn that both Joyce and Gerry were teachers. They had taken early retirement after a stressful profession had affected Gerry's health and found Joyce disillusioned, with an education system that left her, as the teacher, with little authority to control a classroom.

Now hundreds of miles away from their old lives, Gerry, originally a science teacher, has turned his massive brain to working out the mathematical equations of construction, happily immersing himself in his new passion for renovating and extending their ancient home. Meanwhile Joyce, just happy to see her husband relax and become his old self again, fills her time at the sewing machine, embellishing their surroundings, with her gift for arts and crafts.

Don't get me wrong! Joyce is feisty and opinionated and her propensity for the use of the word 'darling' in every sentence can be irritating, but on the whole, the ambience of this beautiful place helps one overlook the idiosyncrasies of our hostess, seeing beneath the surface a caring, intrinsically kind, individual. As we sip our drinks, conversation turns to the often intensely hot days of summer and how we cope with them. Ron and I admit the only way we have found is to jump into a cool shower twice a day. Having come to terms with the fact that our dwindling funds rule out the possibility of a swimming pool in the near future.

Gerry, who has said little up to now, takes a long cool sip of his rosé and, leaning back in his rattan chair, looks earnestly over at Ronnie and exclaims, "What you two need, old chap, is a 'blue blot' on the landscape!' We gave in to one just last month and have never looked back."

Now, as you might have guessed, it is Joyce who is responsible for renaming inanimate objects and it turns out, 'a blue blot on the landscape,' is, in fact, how she refers to the large circular blue plastic swimming pools, dotted around the French countryside.

Joyce goes on to explain how each evening before dinner, they can be found bobbing about in their 'blue blot', which at thirteen feet across and five feet deep can actually facilitate a degree of swimming. " It's an absolute Godsend, darling!" she exudes. " Follow me and I'll show you what I mean!"

Taking a winding path through waist high plants and shrubs, Joyce leads us under a wooden archway, heavy with ancient scented climbing roses, whose huge pink heads, look like they have been splattered with scarlet ink, to an expanse of lawn that lies to the left of the property.

"Here we are darlings." She, announces, as we find ourselves looking over the side of the huge 'blue blot' into a pool of invitingly clear water, sparkling enticingly in the early evening sunshine. Reaching over the side, I run my hand over the surface and, in the silence, the gentle splashes interrupt the sound of nature and the cool water promises relief from the hot balmy air. To one side a white ladder calls out, "Climb in!"

At once, Ron and I realise we are staring at the answer to surviving the long hot days of summer and the good news being, it looks like something we can afford.

Gerry, in his element, describes in great detail the mechanics of setting up your own 'blue blot', specifying the careful addition of fluoride to the water and the daily testing to ensure the levels remain correct. Ron listens intently, as Joyce and I wander off to admire their vegetable plot, another testimony to Gerry's enthusiasm for hard work!

Eventually we manage to extricate ourselves, as Joyce finally stops to draw breath and in a flurry of hugs and enthusiastic cries of, "We must do this again soon, darlings!" We hop in the car and head off up the lane, closely followed by Sybil and Thorny, who provide us with a barking entourage until we reach the road.

So, where do you find us on Monday afternoon? Yes, you are right, in the 'BricoMarché' choosing our very own 'blue blot!' Later as we drive home in the car, the massive box obscures the view from the rear window, but inside, Ron and I, like two children on their way to the seaside, can't wait to get it home.

Over the last few months, so much has been spent on boring things, like paint and wallpaper, this feels like a treat for ourselves and I don't think we could be more excited today, if we were getting a real pool!

Back at the presbytery, impatience sets in, as the installation of the 'blue blot' takes longer than expected. First of all, we have to locate the site and then to make sure the ground is even, a layer of sand must be put down to provide a level base.

Let's just say it is now Tuesday afternoon and the hosepipe is finally in position, as Ron gives the signal to fill her up. The miracle that is clean water flows in and the supporting walls of the pool gradually begin to rise before our eyes, until we too find ourselves, the proud owners of our very own, 'blue blot on the landscape,' carefully concealed in a shady corner of the garden, where our splashing about should hopefully go unnoticed by the neighbours!

And so at six o'clock on a scorchingly hot summer's evening, Ron and I sneak down the garden in our swimsuits, climb the rather wobbly white ladder and land with a splash in the icy cold water. Squealing and floundering, swimming and splashing, we laugh like children!

Chapter Twenty

Nut Wine – with a Kick Like a Mule!

Saturday morning comes around again and our day starts with breakfast on the terrace to the left of the steps, where an overhanging tree provides some welcome shade from the already building heat. A smell of coffee hangs in the still morning air and the gentle tones of radio 4 whisper in the background. Beside me, Murphy sniffs around the flowerbeds stopping transfixed by a busy bumblebee, as it pushes its furry body deep within the petals of a nearby flower and on the steps up to the house, a lizard basks unnoticed on the warm stone.

To the far side of the stone wall at the other end of the garden, I can hear Henri and Chantal, getting on with family life and I find myself hoping they are too busy to notice our tranquil start to the day.

Alas, no sooner has the thought crossed my mind, than I spot Amélie climbing on the garden gate and waving, "Bonjour!" Ron and I wave back and smile, returning to our coffee, in the hope that something more exciting may catch her attention, only to hear her call out, "Papa! C'est Ronnie et Hezzer. Je veux jouer avec Murphy!"

There is just enough time for Ron and I to swap a withering glance, as we wave goodbye to peace and tranquillity and head over to the gate, to pass the time of day with our lovely, but somewhat ever present neighbours!

Henri bounces up in a tight vest and shorts, never missing an opportunity to show off his carefully honed biceps and is, as usual, full of enthusiasm. The excitement today seems to be focused around the completion of some home improvements and after a few moments, he is eager we should follow him inside, where we can cast an eye over his excellent handiwork.

And so, as Ron and Henri walk off towards his house, closely followed by Amélie, eager to hold Ron's hand, I grab Murphy and running up the steps to the presbytery, send the basking lizard scurrying for cover. Depositing a bewildered looking dog in the hallway and closing the door I set off back down the garden towards the gate. As I go I glance across at the breakfast table, where it rests below the branches of the shady tree and notice a wasp helping itself to the marmalade on my half eaten croissant!

Inside the darkness of Henri's kitchen, I find Ron chatting to Chantal, who seems unfazed by this early morning invasion of her home. At almost six foot tall, she looks down lovingly at Henri, her eyes lingering admiringly over his biceps, as she explains how delighted she is with her new luxury bathroom.

Before we are to inspect the bathroom, however, Henri insists we visit his cellar. Leading us all down some stone steps, he proudly takes us through a curtain of long clear plastic strips, designed, Henri explains, to keep the draught of the cellar from entering the house and obtained as a freebie from a butcher friend of his, who had been using it for his meat freezer.

On entering the cellar we pass through the plastic curtain, with its rather dubious stains and find ourselves in a somewhat cluttered space, with a bit of natural light, coming from a horizontal narrow window at street level. In the middle of the floor, a pile of weights and a long iron bar, lie next to some dumb bells and on the beam above, a pole has been fixed, a few feet above our heads.

Henri explains it is here in the cool of the cellar, that he builds the perfect body and with that he leaps into the air and crossing his arms above his head, proceeds to hang, cross-armed from the metal bar. I can't help at this point but make the connection between Henri and the bats we found hanging in a similar fashion in our old barn, but I try not to look amused, as Henri explains in all sincerity, that this is how he builds his strength to take care of such a young wife!

The conversation continues as we await his return to the upright position. He doesn't seem in a hurry, however, and still hanging from the rafters, reminds us again, how he and Chantal met at the Judo class in Petit Villefranche, where he as the teacher had obtained 'Black Belt' status and Chantal was his gifted student.

Ron and I, not quite sure at this moment, exactly how to converse with an upside down person, tilt our heads slightly to one side, as we acknowledge his achievements in the field of Judo and the romantic setting, in which their love had blossomed.

It wasn't all plain sailing, however, he goes on to say. His wife at the time, and mother of his two sons, was very bitter and throughout the divorce proceedings, always referred to Chantal as "Le Cheval." Well, even from his inverted position, it is possible to see from Henri's face that the comparison of Chantal with a horse had been painful to listen to. Acknowledging now, with a sigh of relief, that it is all in the past, Henri returns to the upright position and gives Chantal a reassuring pat on the bottom, followed by a quick ripple of his bulging biceps.

Leading us from the cellar, he points out amongst the piles of bric-à-brac some items of particular interest he has picked up from local 'Brocantes.' It soon becomes clear that Henri will never buy anything new, if he can find it in a junk shop. We are not talking priceless antiques here, I hasten to add, but rather items that time and good taste have long forgotten, but as we are about to find out, reappear in Henri's efforts at DIY!

Returning to the kitchen, he points out a staircase and explains that it takes you up to his bedroom and a small adjacent room, where Amélie sleeps. It is not this staircase we are taking today, however, as apparently there is no access to the family bathroom from their bedroom. We dutifully follow Henri through the kitchen and into the lounge, where another staircase is

139

demonstrated, which leads to the 'nouvelle salle des bains' and an unfinished guest room, intended for his sons, when they come to stay.

Climbing the stairs, he admits the only major hiccup in his plan so far, is his inability to solve the problem of joining his bedroom and Amélie's, to the 'nouvelle' bathroom. There would appear to be a thick structural wall between the two, which is beyond Henri's DIY skills, leaving them with an intrepid hike to the bathroom, should nature call during the night. Finally, at the top of the second staircase, off a small landing, Chantal is the first to run ahead and excitedly open the door of the new luxury convenience. Ron and I peer into the spacious room in front of us, with its shiny glass shower cubicle and taking a quick glance around, find all necessary sanitary equipment to be present and correct and the overall first impression to be good, "C'est jolie, Chantal, très jolie!" we chorus in unison.

Chantal beams with pride as Henri squeezes past her, eager to fill us in on the cost cutting features of the luxury facility, as our eyes begin to focus closer on the detail of the finish.

He commences by pointing out two wall lights above the sink, that he had been storing in the cellar. Installing them hadn't been easy, he goes on to say and closer inspection of the brass fixtures reveal the indents of a hammer, where he has tried valiantly to nail them to the wall. Reaching up to adjust the shade on one, it shifts precariously to the right and remaining there, flickers intermittently.

Quickly moving on from the feature lighting, he draws our attention to the 'carrelage' or tiling, which he considers to be one of his better skills. True enough the plain white tiles give the space a contemporary feel, but on closer inspection, the normally straight lines between the tiles, appear to lead off at an angle, which after a few minutes, have the effect of rendering one slightly disorientated. The whole bathroom now giving the sensation of stepping into a surrealist painting by Salvador Dali!

140

Chantal, however, is oblivious to her luxury bathroom's little foibles and hasn't even noticed the two mismatched taps on the basin, both bearing the instruction 'froid' on the top! With great pride, she declares, " Mon mari, il est formidable!" With that Henri straightens the loose towel rail and, closing the door behind us, carefully conceals the knob in his pocket, to replace later!

Back in the kitchen, Chantal produces tiny cups of espresso for everyone and we sit around the table chatting. Henri talks about his work as a lorry driver and explains about the sideline, both he and Chantal have been fostering for over a year now, where they provide catering for functions and weddings.

The new enterprise takes up a lot of their spare time, but is something they both enjoy and, like every French person I have ever met, their passion for food is part of their identity and an opportunity to work in the field of 'catering', would seem an obvious path to pursue.

They go on, in whispered tones, to say how they have their eyes fixed on the boulangerie across the street. The proprietors there leave a lot to be desired, a strange couple I have mentioned before in passing. Madame Edith Lebert, who lives in the back of the shop, always seems reluctant to come out to serve customers. When she is forced to, it is written all over her face that you have interrupted her favourite French game show, the demented sounds of which spill out of her 'Séjour' into the shop beyond.

There is little on the shelves, bar some random tins of food and behind the counter a few lonely baguettes line the wall. Henri relates to us how she keeps the fresh baguettes for her chosen friends and furnishes the other customers with ones she has stashed in her freezer for months. This would explain the chewy tough texture of her bread, which has proved a challenge to our molars, on the odd occasion when I have been forced to visit the establishment.

Frank, her husband, a burly man with a huge black beard, sits on a wooden chair outside the shop, watching the world go by. Inside, above the shelves of tins, a row of magazines bearing the odd titles of, "Men in Big Boots!" would appear to be centred round some rather unsavoury topics and have caused many young mothers in the village to refuse to bring their children into the shop at all.

Chantal has heard on the grapevine that they can't afford to run the business for much longer and Henri would be keen to take over. Eagerly she describes how they would bake bread on the premises daily and fill the empty shelves with all kinds of delicious pâtisserie.

Ron and I encourage them along, relishing the idea of the smell of freshly baked bread each morning and the convenience of being able to visit our boulangerie, without having to get past the ominous figure of bearded Frank in the doorway and running the gauntlet past the unsavoury magazines, only to be met by Edith with her face like thunder!

In the back of my mind, I do find myself hoping Henri's baking skills are better than his DIY skills, but I quickly put this thought to one side, having already sampled some of his culinary delights and, not only living to tell the tale, I must confess to having been pleasantly surprised.

Just when Ron and I are about to try and extricate ourselves and get on with the day, it suddenly looks like I won't have to wait that long, before getting the opportunity to evaluate Henri's cooking skills, yet again. As Ron pushes his chair back to get up, Chantal mentions that 'The Parisians' arrived in Saint-Allier last night, for the month of August and have taken up residence in their holiday home, a bungalow with a small swimming pool, just across the road.

You must meet them enthuses Henri, as he invites us to join them for a barbeque later in the day and so, eager by now to get out the door, we agree to return at around six o'clock, for apéros and a barbeque, with the afore-mentioned Parisians.

Having shared three kisses each, we take our leave and heading back to the garden, stop to clear the table. Switching off radio 4, I empty the remains of our tranquil breakfast into a black plastic bag and, climbing the steps to release Murphy, begin to reorganise the day around our evening invitation.

In the afternoon, I call in to the florist in Petit Villefranche, where outside an array of rather gaudily wrapped plants, bedecked in brightly coloured cellophane, wait patiently to be purchased and presented to the hostess of one of the many 'Saturday night Soirées' taking place around the village.

Finally, I settle for a red flower, nestling deep within it's cellophane wrapper and tied with a red ribbon; the florist wishes me a 'Bonne Soirée!' and I return to the presbytery, just in time to have a shower and change for the evening.

Looking around everywhere for Ron, I finally find him at the bottom of the garden beside the 'blue blot,' where, standing transfixed by the sparkling water of the pool, he slowly skims off flies from the surface, lost in a world of his own. "Sorry to interrupt, darling, but isn't it time you were changed? I can see smoke rising from Henri's barbeque!"

I watch him return to the house and, taking his place by the pool, gaze over the edge into the clear blue water. At the other side, a coloured moth catches my attention, as it struggles on the surface and, grabbing the net, I set out on a rescue mission. Lifting it gently from the water, I carefully lower the tiny creature onto the grass, where it rests, stretching its delicate multicoloured wings out to dry, in the evening sunshine.

Ten minutes later, Ron re-appears, hair still damp from the shower, but sporting a clean red T-shirt and shorts and carrying the now colour co-ordinated, cellophane wrapped gift for Chantal. Simultaneously we greet each other with a, "Bonne Soirée!" and laughing, set off through the gate, hand in hand to our barbeque, unaware that back by the pool, the little coloured moth spreads its carefully dried wings and flutters off into the night.

Stepping into Henri's garden, we make our way to the patio, where a long white plastic table stretches the length of the terrace. Casting my eye around, it seems Parisians are everywhere! In the corner I can just make out Henri, holding forth by the barbeque. "C'est les Irlandais!", he announces with great gusto, gesturing to us to come and join him, eager to show off the new neighbours to his friends from Paris.

Introductions all round reveal a large family, with the unusual 'Nom de Famille' of Monsieur et Madame Canard. They have been escaping to the countryside here in Saint-Allier every August since their children were small and now, at least twenty-five years on, their grown-up daughters, respective husbands and a number of grandchildren accompany them.

With the arrival of 'Old Jacques' and Françoise, Henri is keen to get the party started and, holding a tray above his head, waiter style, he balances a bottle of his famous 'Nut Wine' and some glasses. As he passes by, I catch Chantal and hand over our colour co-ordinated cellophane gift, which she greets with much enthusiasm, before carefully parking it on the kitchen table, alongside several other cellophane wrapped works of art, concealing varying forms of horticultural life.

The 'Nut Wine' I notice is receiving a great reception amongst the men of our party, who greet it with cries of bravo and exclamations of "Oh la la! C'est fort!" Having been caught out before by home made alcoholic French drinks, I make a silent vow to ask for a Pineau, as behind me I hear Henri go on to describe how the walnuts are soaked in 'Eau de Vie' or pure alcohol over the winter months, to produce this rustic French beverage, with a kick like a mule!

Out of the corner of my eye, I can't help but notice Ron, eager to be 'one of the lads' is already halfway through his first glass and is joining in manfully to extol the virtues of this year's vintage. Meanwhile, I accept a Pineau from Chantal, who exchanges a knowing glance with me, as we both silently agree, "Boys will be boys!"

144

Chatting away to Monsieur Canard and his son in law, Maurice, I notice the younger ladies of the family seem less happy to come over and say hello and I can tell the language barrier is the most likely problem. From past experience, I realise they have discovered it hard to maintain their Parisian chic, while getting sentences back to front and pronunciation way off the mark. Therefore, although curious, they would rather remain at a safe distance, their essential poise still intact.

So, as we take our places at the table, I find myself next to Ron and on the other side, Monsieur Canard, who, like all French men, soon forgets the language barrier, when confronted with the chance to chat up a mysterious, foreign female.

Nut wine is yet again topped up, as Chantal sends bowls of clear consommé down the long table. The soup is a firm favourite with the French, as it cleanses the palate and prepares one's taste buds for what is to come. Tucking in, Henri calls out for each person's preferred 'cuissance,' as he busily cooks the steaks to order, his gleaming biceps reflecting in the light from the glowing barbeque!

Dusk begins to fall and, above our heads, bats wheel and turn in the night sky; the smoke rises from Henri's barbeque and, over the buzz of conversation, frogs and crickets perform their evening chorus.

Glancing at Ron, I turn back to Monsieur Canard, as he continues his attempt to impress me, with the intricate details of his job in the city, but then I double back to Ron. In the lamplight of the terrace, I notice he has turned a strange colour.

"Are you all right?" I whisper. At first there is no reply, so I try again. "Ron, what is it, you look like death warmed up?" "I'm sorry, Heather. I've got to go home. It's the 'Nut Wine'! I think I am going to be sick!" As he excuses himself from the table and heads off in the direction of the presbytery, his last words to me are, "Stay and cover for me!"

Suddenly there is an empty space to my right and in my head time stands still. What do I say, worse still, how do I say it in

French? It is not long before people notice Ron's sudden departure and Chantal is the first to ask, "Où est Ronnie?" The only words that come to mind on the spur of the moment are, "Desolée, il est malade, je pense!" Not what everyone wants to hear, while seated round the dinner table and poor Henri, disappointed at the loss of his star attraction, lets his spatula drop to the ground, with a resounding clunk!

The delicious steaks, cooked to perfection, arrive on our plates and salads and crusty bread are passed around. Gradually conversation returns to normal and Monsieur Canard resumes where he left off. Alas, I find it really hard to concentrate, wondering if Ron will return, while still trying to understand the stream of French flowing into my left ear.

Eventually, dessert arrives in the form of slices of pear Torte and by now I realise I am on my own. Ron is not returning and valiantly I try to fend off all enquiries, as to what has happened to him. Inside, I think, how can he just abandon me like this? And so, as the situation becomes clear, I set about dreaming up an escape plan.

Monsieur Canard is beginning to become bored of trying to chat me up, as I no doubt look somewhat distracted, so finding a lull in the conversation, I take my opportunity and declare that I ought to say, "Bonne Nuit" and, "Chercher Ronnie." Getting up to leave the table, I share three kisses with a rather confused looking Chantal and Henri, and thanking them for a lovely meal, I make my escape into the night!

Stealing back through the gates of the presbytery, I notice that the ground floor of the house is in darkness and climbing the steps in the moonlight, I open the front door and call out, "Ronnie!" Silence, and then in the distance, I can just make out a faint groan. Heading up the stairs, past a sleeping Murphy in his basket, my attention is drawn to a shaft of light coming from the 'Grande salle des bains' and pushing the door open, there in the semi-darkness, stands the dejected figure of my husband. With

146

little strength left to speak, I barely make out through the silence his faint whimper, "I think I've been kicked by a mule!"

Chapter Twenty-One

Not Murphy's Finest Hour

Throwing open the shutters, which creak their welcome to a new day and looking out over the park, I see sunlight begin to burn off the early morning mist, casting shadows across the terrace below. I watch as Ron erects the parasol in an effort to create a shady retreat where we can enjoy coffee later; thankfully, he can once again contemplate food having recovered from his excess of nut wine and has willingly agreed to take the pledge regarding that particular alcoholic beverage. Indeed, as I prepare to return the hospitality of our new friends, Joyce and Gerry, unbeknown to myself, it is not Ron I have to worry about, but a certain young terrier named Murphy who is about to 'blot his copybook'!
Outside in the heat of the afternoon, the table and parasol sit unused as I spend my day in the kitchen preparing food for our guests. I work hard, as I really want to thank Joyce and Gerry for their introduction to the 'blue blot', which has transformed our ability to cope with the heat around here. On the cooker, a large pot of chilli simmers gently as I wash the crisp lettuce under icy water. Looking out the kitchen window, it is hard not to notice Ron has taken up position under the parasol, a newspaper spread out in front of him on the table, while below, Murphy lies on his back, all four paws in the air.
Eventually, with everything under control I prepare to head off for a shower before our guests arrive. On leaving the kitchen, I lean out the window and peering through an array of red geraniums at the tranquil scene below, I have to admit to a modicum of delight

as I call time on their relaxation. "Ron, could you possibly set the table in the dining room for me? Oh, and replace that newspaper with some wine and nibbles under the parasol!" Skipping up the stairs in the direction of the shower, I ignore the protestations of, " In a minute dear. Just finishing this article."

It is Murphy who announces the eventual arrival of Joyce and Gerry as their four-wheel drive roars through the gates in a cloud of dust, before drawing up at the foot of the steps. Ron, first to greet them, helps Joyce down from the elevated passenger seat, without the aid of a ladder, prompting one to wonder why they would choose a mode of transport that surely must require a hoist to get her in? Gerry, on the other hand has no problem and leaps down, sandals first, from the driver's seat.

Around us, the stillness of the evening resounds to Joyce's cries of, "Bonjour, darling!" So lovely to see you again," while the ensuing rise of excitement levels unfortunately whip Murphy up into a bit of a frenzy and he joins in the fun, barking and wagging his tail as he circles the welcome party.

Joyce and Gerry are well used to dogs and, having left Sybil and Thorny at home for the evening, reward Murphy with some hearty petting. Calmness eventually returns and I invite all assembled to a seat under the parasol, where Ron has dutifully uncorked a chilled bottle of Rose. This is, of course, Joyce and Gerry's first visit '*chez nous*' and the chat soon turns to gardens, as I pick her brains on horticultural matters. I notice, like her beautiful cottage garden, Joyce has chosen a magnificent floral number in lilac this evening, which perfectly matches her vivacious personality. Next to her, Gerry's khaki shorts, socks and sandals perhaps suggest an English man abroad, but belie the fact that this is one English man not afraid to get his hands dirty.

While he enthusiastically describes in great detail his latest renovation project, i.e. opening up the wall into an out-house to lovingly create their new dining room, Murphy lies at his feet, to all intents and purposes, the perfect lap dog and gradually the conversation turns to pets.

149

Joyce and Gerry glaze over, as they lovingly describe how they purchased their two Shih Tzus seven years earlier from an accredited breeder back home in England. Since then, Sybil and Thorny have conducted themselves impeccably, never putting a paw wrong, and, as we are to find out later, have perhaps lulled their devoted owners into a false sense of security around other people's furry friends!

I take the opportunity at this point, as I always do with visitors, to advise caution with Murphy. He is the most adorable fluffy white West Highland terrier you could meet and a faithful companion to whom I have a very strong bond. Indeed, he rarely takes his eyes off me and is always aware of my whereabouts as he trots around after me. I go on to explain, however, that he is a very nervous dog due to a less fortunate start in life than Sybil and Thorny.

Joyce and Gerry listen interestedly, as I go on to explain how Murphy had been advertised in our local paper back in Belfast. Naively, I didn't recognise the warning signs. The advert stated several breeds of pup for sale, which I later learned is often the sign of a 'puppy farm'. Delighted to find a puppy locally, however, my daughter, Katie and I jumped into the car armed with my chequebook and a warm blanket for our new charge. Winding our way along the country road, just a couple of miles outside town, we shortly arrived at the address in the advert.

Set back from the road, we were confronted with a rather run down looking farmhouse with a couple of very dilapidated outbuildings. The whole place was surrounded by what can only be described as a dumping ground for old rusty scrap metal and any other unwanted debris one could imagine. As the adult in the situation, (Katie was about thirteen at the time), I knew at once I should turn the car and head for home. We were both so keen to get our new puppy, however, and against my better judgement, I pulled into the derelict yard in front of the house, to the sound of barking dogs and the terrified clucking of a couple of scruffy looking chickens.

Almost a little afraid, I approached the door and, before I could knock, was met by a large woman in a less than pristine housecoat, whose enormous frame filled the doorway. I stated the reason for our presence and she mumbled there was only one Westie left and two Shih Tzus, but to follow her if I was still interested. Choosing our steps carefully, we accompanied her across the mucky yard in the direction of one of the dilapidated outhouses, to a building that contained no windows, as far as I could see.

Throwing open the top half of a rickety stable door, Katie and I peered into the darkness. Below us, two little Shih Tzu pups ran towards the door, their big brown eyes blinking against the light, while in the background, a dirty little white bundle cowered in the corner and I knew at once we had to rescue him!

Returning home in the car, Katie clutched our bedraggled little puppy close to her. At the vets the next day, our suspicions were confirmed; little Murphy had come from a puppy farm. He was not initially from the awful farm where we found him, but according to his pedigree, from an address some 200 miles away in Southern Ireland. He was covered in fleas and his skin was itchy and sore; the vet reckoned he was also too young to be separated from his mother. Who can tell what he suffered during the long journey, until finally abandoned in that dark, outhouse, but he was very wary of people and any sudden movement would cause him to cower in fear.

With love and affection over the next months, Murphy recovered physically from his awful neglect and became the loving pet he is today, but he has always remained nervous with strangers and, as I finish my story, I advise Joyce and Gerry to be careful, as he can be a bit unpredictable if frightened. Joyce seems to get the message at once and appears happy to admire Murphy from afar. Gerry, on the other hand, lands an almighty pat on our unsuspecting pooch's back and declares, "Oh, there's no problem! Murphy and I are mates. He loves his uncle Gerry!"

Heading for the kitchen to attend to the food, I glance back at Murphy, thinking to myself that I am not sure if it is love I see in his eyes, rather an element of mistrust and, as Gerry bursts out into raucous laughter at one of his own jokes, Murphy moves to safer ground and joins me in the kitchen.

Together he keeps me company, as I put the finishing touches to the starter. Meanwhile, upstairs I can hear Ronnie giving our guests a tour of the house and Joyce's enthusiastic endorsements of, "Oh, it's lovely, darling!" echo down the winding staircase, punctuated by Gerry's loud bursts of laughter, each of which causes Murphy to fidget nervously.

By now, I am busy placing the first course on the table and eventually, lighting a candle to add to the ambiance, I invite everyone to assemble for supper. Around the table, conversation is animated as we tuck into our starter of cool smoked salmon. Joyce is the most talkative, her enthusiasm sometimes leaving it difficult to get a word in edgeways, while Gerry, with his six foot three frame and booming voice, has no trouble being heard over the assembled company. Manfully, I try to hold my own in the conversation, as Ron attempts to keep Gerry's glass topped up, a job that is seemingly becoming a full time task!

The meal goes down well and having finally polished off dessert, we each lean back in our seats and enjoy a moment of relaxation, as even Joyce pauses to draw breath. Reaching over to the sideboard, Ron retrieves a bottle of Cognac and suggests a '*digestif*', an offer which Joyce and I decline graciously, leaving a rather red-nosed Gerry to exclaim, "Yum! Yes, please!"

Around the table, the scene is set. In the light of a now spluttering candle, cheeks are rosy and the atmosphere is jovial, while underneath, unbeknown to myself, Murphy forages amongst a sea of legs for any leftover crumbs. Gerry, first to become aware of the presence below table, mainly due to his lack of trousers, announces with great gusto, " Is that my old friend, Murphy?" Meanwhile, Joyce, unable to hide a note of irritation with her somewhat inebriated husband, repeats my instruction to give Murphy a wide berth. Alas! Her protestations fall on deaf ears, as

Gerry disappears under the table to the immortal words, " Just call me the dog whisperer!"

One can only imagine how the appearance of Gerry's upturned head amongst the sea of legs would look to our unsuspecting mutt, but with our guest's red nose only inches from Murphy's face, the ensuing growl says it all! Above table, we have just enough time to glance horrified at each other before Gerry resurfaces. Still grinning from ear to ear, due to the anaesthetising effect of the cognac, his rapidly swelling red nose now spouts blood, like a fountain, down the front of his open necked khaki shirt.

Our tranquil dinner party is instantly thrown into chaos. Joyce, leaping to her feet, reprimands Gerry for his stupidity, whilst desperately trying to stem the flow of blood with one of my National Trust floral napkins. Meanwhile, I try to ignore Ronnie, as he disappears stage left with our disgraced mutt still growling under one arm. In the kitchen beyond, I can just make out the threatening sound of my husband's voice as he gives the command, " Bad dog! Into bed!"

The remainder of the evening is transformed into a scene from a Red Cross training seminar, as I attempt to bandage Gerry's throbbing nose. At last, helping our rather shocked guests down the steps to their car, Ronnie and I apologise profusely for our pet's behaviour and Joyce, eventually ensconced in the driver's seat, calls out, "Bonsoir, darling!" as she sets off into the night. Beside her, the pale ghostly figure of the 'dog whisperer' stares out from the passenger seat and, passing the kitchen where Murphy sleeps innocently curled up in his basket, Ron and I agree, " It wasn't his finest hour!"

Chapter Twenty-Two

Pierre Gabin doesn't disappoint!

A busy week commences towards the end of August, with the arrival this morning of our long awaited painter, Pierre Gabin. We first contacted Pierre back in April, when he informed us, like any other painter worth his salt in the region, he had a waiting list a kilometre long, but insisted he would be happy to add us to it. So, early this morning, after a phone-call at the weekend, the long awaited Pierre arrives and, jumping out of his van at the bottom of the presbytery steps, he certainly isn't a disappointment!

Six foot tall and in his early forties, Pierre Gabin, is dressed in slim-fitting casual trousers and an immaculately ironed white shirt. His dark hair is slicked back and, opening the door to greet him, I find myself unwittingly seduced, by the allure of his expensive cologne. Formalities having been exchanged, we discuss the job in hand, which entails him removing and refurbishing all the shutters, before painting them a delightful pale green colour and replacing them on either side of each window.

Sneaking another quick peak at Pierre's ensemble, I find myself wondering, just how he is going to achieve this, without ruining his debonair appearance. Monsieur Gabin is a professional, however, and I need not have worried, as eager to get started the job, he bounces down the steps to his van, where all is revealed shall we say, in more ways than one!

Through the kitchen window, I just happen to notice, Pierre open the back door of the van and lift out a neat pile of sparkling white overalls, which he places on the stone pillar at the bottom of the steps. Next he slowly unbuttons the crisp white shirt, to reveal a slim tanned body underneath and casually stretching in the still fresh morning air, steps effortlessly into his work ensemble. A vision in white is revealed, for which it is almost necessary to reach for ones sunglasses!

My attention is drawn back into the moment by the sound of footsteps on the stairs, as I realise my Dad, who having been put on a plane from Southampton the day before by my sister, is emerging to start the day. In his eighties, Dad is somewhat set in his ways, although, so far, we have managed to recreate his perfect breakfast, by stocking up on lashings of marmalade and semi-skimmed milk. The challenge doesn't end there, however, as I am soon to find out!

"How about nipping out for coffee and a scone, Heather?" he chirps up happily, on entering the kitchen. "We could pick up the morning paper." "Nice idea, Dad, but I am not sure about scones. I don't think they go in for them so much here. Would you settle for a croissant?" "What! No scones?", he exclaims in disbelief. "How can you have a coffee shop without scones?" At this he shuffles off through the open door, in the direction of the garden to inspect the plants, mumbling to himself regarding the sanity of a country bereft of the aforementioned confectionery. In the kitchen, meanwhile, I make a mental note to self, "Google, the perfect scone recipe!"

Deciding the safest thing to do, is to put the kettle on and have coffee here, where at least I can guarantee a recognisable Digestive biscuit, I set the tray ready to take out to the garden and call out to Monsieur Gabin through the open window, "Un Café, Monsieur?" Monsieur Gabin replies, "It isn't the right time for coffee!" This is something I have heard from French artisans before, although I haven't quite worked out exactly when the right time is. At least I didn't offer him a cup of tea, I think to myself, which I have been reliably informed, has other connotations!

Later in the morning, I drive Dad to Petit Villefranche, where we stop at the newsagent's to pick up his paper. I did explain to him, the papers would be a day late here, but it seems he has forgotten and, on the journey home, the air of disappointment in the car is palpable. "This news is out of date, Heather. How can I keep up to date, if the news is out of date?" "Well Dad. I think you'll find, that the whole fun of living here is that the pace of life doesn't depend on keeping up to date with the news. If anything, the French countryside is still about twenty years behind Britain and a more peaceful place for it."

Dad, beginning to get the idea now, leans back in his seat and smiles, " It's a bit like 'the good old days' you mean?" "Yes, a bit like 'the good old days' Dad." And as if to prove my point, driving back into Saint-Allier and turning right into the lane, we meet Françoise wielding a brown paper bag and waving frantically. Pulling the car up beside her, I wind down the window and introduce her to Dad. Smiling from ear to ear, she hands over her brown paper parcel, "Pour vous, Monsieur! Des fèves!" she exclaims with delight and, as we look inside, I realise she has remembered, I told her Dad loved broad beans and she has picked him a bagful from her 'potager'.

Back at the house, Monsieur Gabin has left for his two-hour lunch. He has already removed all the shutters from the back of the house and looking into the barn, his 'Atelier' is as immaculate as the man himself. In the kitchen, I rustle up a salad and shelling some of the broad beans, sprinkle them over the top. Dad is thrilled that Françoise has remembered his passion for the noble bean and is beginning to feel quite at home, as he, Ron and I, share a delightful lunch together around the kitchen table rather than outside under the midday sun.

After lunch, when the dishes are cleared, we chat about the afternoon and what Dad would like to do. On the sideboard in the hall, a card sits next to the antique clock we bought at a

'Brocante' in Angoulême. It's an invitation to an Art exhibition, to be held in the garden of the artist, a Monsieur Jean-Luc Persyn. One is invited to browse through his latest offerings, while sipping a glass of chilled wine.

After some discussion, Dad decides to stay behind and retire to his room with the paper. We all agree this is probably for the best, as the afternoon sun has been really hot recently and besides, tonight we have arranged to take him for a meal, in the Château restaurant at Petit Villefranche, which is always a special treat.

Ron and I leave Dad ensconced in the lovely back bedroom, with its blue toile wallpaper and his own little television. At the foot of his bed Murphy lies curled up asleep, as the two share an afternoon siesta. Driving through the gates, we pass Pierre Gabin on his way in; he is once again wearing the crisp white shirt and, as he winds down his window to wish us a, "Bonne Journée!", the unmistakable sound of 'Johnny Halliday' drifts out from within, mixed with the intoxicating aroma of his seductive aftershave!

Driving along roads through the French countryside, we pass tiny villages shuttered against the afternoon heat, bereft of any signs of life. Rolling fields of sunflowers stretch out on either side of us and, inside the car, we chat about the exhibition we are about to see.

Jean-Luc Persyn is a young artist, introduced to us by Mike O'Casey, who rather like an art patron of old, has a passion for the artist's work and has bought many of his paintings, which now adorn the walls of 'Belles Côtes.' Jean-Luc paints in oils, specialising in still life and taking his inspiration from the old masters, his work has a rich depth of colour and a wonderful use of light and shade. With my birthday imminent, Dad has very kindly suggested, he would help me out, if I saw something I liked.

Just before we arrive at Jean-Luc's, we pass through the pretty village of St Laurent. Perched on the side of a valley, the houses are tiered down the hill, each one clinging to the side, their balconies looking out over the view beyond, bedecked with trailing Geraniums. St Laurent is what they call in France a 'Ville Fleurie', the title given to the prettiest villages, renowned for their floral displays and picturesque settings and St Laurent doesn't disappoint.

Driving around the square, brightly coloured bars and restaurants fill the air with aromatic smells of garlic and freshly brewed coffee and, at its heart, ancient shady trees provide a lush green canopy for the brightly coloured tables below. Being the summer, the little square provides an idyllic spot for tourists, who, delighted to stumble upon such a tranquil place, sip coffee or an ice-cold beer in its welcome shade.

Today, we don't stop, however, as just a few miles outside St Laurent, we arrive at the tiny hamlet of Bainac and, as the map on the back of the invitation suggests, passing through the hamlet, we come across a hand made sign pointing up a lane. The sign reads 'Exposition d'Art.'

The end of the lane opens into a small, rather overgrown field, where several cars are parked under the shade of some overhanging trees. On the other side of a hedge, the roof of a tiny cottage is just visible. Making our way around the front of the cottage into a clearing, we are met by several small marquees, one serving wine and nibbles and the others providing seating for around twenty or thirty intrepid art lovers. The scene itself is one of colourful jollity and, with the addition of a few ladies sporting parasols, would be reminiscent of a painting by Monet!

Making our way over to the wine tent, Ron and I help ourselves to a glass of chilled rosé and, on turning around, catch the welcoming eye of Mike and Maeve O'Casey, who call us to join them at their table. As I have mentioned before, the O'Caseys consider themselves to be patrons of Jean-Luc and have, as such, been here since early morning, helping set up the exhibition and encouraging art lovers to part with their hard earned cash.

It soon becomes apparent, though, that it has been a long tiring day for them both, helped out in no small way by the copious amounts of alcohol they have kindly donated to the free bar and, by now, Mike and Maeve are both shall we say rather merry! As Mike regales us with some of his wonderful Irish humour, I find myself pondering his very red nose and wonder if it is a result of the sun, or the inevitable outcome of his own bounteous hospitality?

Reluctant to leave the fun, but curious to see Jean-Luc's work, we excuse ourselves from the table and, as Mike calls out after us, "Enjoy the exhibition! C'est super-bon!" in his lovely Irish accent, we duck down and enter the cottage through a low door, concealed under an overhanging vine, heavy with dark purple grapes.

Inside, one room of the cottage has been set up as a gallery and the walls painted white. Everywhere canvasses hang from the white walls, some also propped up against each other in piles on the floor and one or two are displayed on easels. Through a doorway I can just make out the figure of Jean-Luc, standing over several works laid out on the kitchen table. His arms wave about dramatically, as he describes in French the inspiration behind each work. Looking past him, the chaos of his living environment spills out from every corner, as the tiny cottage reveals the penniless life of a struggling artist is no different today, than it ever was.

I have seen Jean-Luc's work exhibited before and the last time my eye had been drawn to a beautiful painting entitled 'Les Pivoines' or in English, 'The Peonies'. A painting in oils, it depicted a vase of peonies with huge, heavy, pink heads, on a table next to a beautifully coloured antique plate. In the Modernist style, its rich colours had caught my attention, but I never expected to see it again.

Scanning the walls now, I pass over various fruit arrangements and some rather strange paintings, depicting cuts of meat, which seem to inspire the artist. Finally, looking up into a shadowy

159

corner of the room, there it is; its vibrant colours putting everything else in the shade, it still fills my heart with delight.

Jean-Luc is quick to give us his attention, when he realises we are genuinely interested in the painting and tells us how he painted it, here in the cottage, during a spell of bad weather, when the peonies sat on a little table by the window and lit up a gloomy corner of the tiny room. He admits the painting is one of his favourites.

And so we emerge into the bright afternoon sunlight, three hundred euros lighter of pocket, but hopefully richer for our first investment in the world of art. We look at each other with a quizzical glance, as we both silently agree we have either made a clever investment, or have just been taken for a couple of mugs! Anyway, whichever it is, I can't wait to get home and find a special place in the presbytery to enjoy my beautiful 'Peonies'.

Mike and Maeve are delighted we are not leaving empty-handed and thank us profusely for coming. Making our way back to the car, I feel we have joined the elite club of 'The Jean-Luc Persyn Appreciation Society', but find myself wondering, if it will ever spread beyond the Charente?

Arriving back at the presbytery around five o'clock, Monsieur Gabin's 'Atelier' is deserted. Glancing in through the open barn doors, I can just make out our shutters, in various stages of refurbishment, neatly stacked against the wall and on his pristine work-bench, a shiny radio patiently awaits his return, to release once again the husky tones of 'Johnny Halliday' to his adoring French public!

Inside the presbytery, we are greeted by what I can only describe as a rather traumatised father. It turns out his siesta has been merciless cut short, due to a series of 'invasions' by the French.

The first intrusion commenced with a knock on the front door, at around three o'clock in the afternoon. Now, Dad would have probably been best to ignore this, but being of the old school, he feels duty bound to answer the call and, making his way down the stairs to the hallway, finds he is unable to open the large, heavy wooden door.

On the other side of the door, Françoise in a state of confusion, calls out instructions in French, which, of course, might as well be 'Double Dutch' and, Dad's subsequent replies in English only serve to confuse the situation even further. Finally, just as a siege mentality is beginning to set in, Françoise comes up with the bright idea of rapping loudly on the dining room window, resulting in poor Dad almost suffering a coronary, before realising what is happening.

On recognising the face at the window from earlier in the day, he manages to open it, only to be met by another barrage of French from the beaming Françoise, as she thrusts yet more broad beans through the aperture into Dad's awaiting hands. Calling out, "Bonne Journée!" she disappears again below the window and slips away in the direction of her potager, leaving a rather stunned Dad in a state of shock, as he slumps down into a nearby chair, under a sea of cascading broad beans!

Having gathered himself together, after his latest French encounter, he manages to make his way into the hall in the direction of the kitchen, with the intent of putting the broad beans safely in the larder, only to be met by the burly figure of yet another unknown Frenchman, this time having entered via the back door, he has already breeched defences.

Yet another barrage of French ensues, valiantly rebuffed by Dad's protestations of, "Je ne parle pas Français!" As it turns out, the intruder is none other than the long awaited Monsieur Fournier, who had promised, two months earlier, to call in and fix the afore-mentioned front door and it would appear nothing is going to deter him from his mission. Eventually Dad, making out the name Kennedy amongst a cacophony of sound, decides, he must know Ronnie and myself and, agreeing to step aside, lets him get on with the job.

Placing the broad beans in the larder, he comes to the conclusion it would be safer outdoors and decides to calm his nerves in the traditional fashion, by inspecting the plants. Descending the steps into the tranquillity of the garden, he realises Monsieur Gabin is safely ensconced in the barn with 'Johnny Halliday' and all is calm.

Finding himself back in the moment, he loses himself in the borders, admiring the plants and allowing his mind to be distracted by the colourful insects, too busy to notice his passing shadow. All is quiet except for the drone of a worker bee, going about its daily business, when the silence is broken yet again, "Bonjour, Monsieur! Je m'appelle Henri, le voisin de Hezzer et Ronnie."

Dad swings round to be met by Henri, a vision in fluorescent orange shorts and a tight black vest. "Ah! Bonjour, Monsieur!", Dad replies, digging deep to draw on his meagre French vocabulary, while all the time thinking to himself, Henri will soon give up, when he realises communication is going to be difficult. Alas for poor Dad, Henri is not easily deterred and continues in French, as if father understands all.

Slowly, Dad starts to walk backwards towards the house, hoping Henri will get the message. Finally, proffering a wave, he takes flight faster than he ever thought possible, up the steps to the relative safety of the hallway. Closing the door behind him, he breathes a sigh of relief and, deciding to lock himself away until our return, heads up to the safety of his blue toile bedroom!

Several hours later, in the car on the way to the Château, Dad manages to laugh, as he relates his encounters with the French, but concludes wryly, that it will be a long time to come, before he volunteers to be 'Home Alone' in the French countryside.

Slowly, the car climbs the narrow, winding streets leading up to the Château and pulls into the car park high above the little village of Petit Villefranche. Getting out of the car, the view is amazing and we stop to look out over the stone wall across the village, to the rolling hills beyond. In the warm early evening air, a faint hint of garlic suggests the gastronomic delights to come.

Linking arms with Dad, Ron leads the way, as we cross the original drawbridge and pass through the thick walls of the Château, into a huge courtyard with tables laid out under the evening sky. From a heavy iron studded wooden door, light pours out onto the cobbles and the figure of Pascal Lambert, the restaurant owner, is silhouetted against the glow, as he awaits his hungry guests, eager to greet them in person.

"Ah! Madame et Monsieur Kennedy. Vous allez bien ce soir?" Pascal embraces us, like long lost friends and as we share three kisses, I introduce Dad, who in turn is welcomed with a warm handshake and some of Pascal's best English, " You are very welcome, sir!"

Ron and I met Pascal shortly after our arrival in Saint-Allier, when we made our first foray to his amazing restaurant, on the recommendation of Susan and James, in whose Gîte we were staying at the time. Pascal was fascinated to hear we had bought the old presbytery in Saint-Allier, as he had viewed the property himself and loved the place. He and his partner, Philippe, went on to purchase another presbytery, in a hamlet just walking distance from the Château and he can't resist the opportunity now, to share renovation stories whenever we meet.

A glamorous figure, at least six feet two tall, Pascal like many French people we have met, has always been intrigued by our surname and seems unable to believe there is no connection with the famous 'American President' despite our protestations. Showing us to our table this evening, his flamboyant side is unable to resist the opportunity to announce across the restaurant, "La carte pour les Kennedys, s'il vous plaît!" Strangely enough, the other French diners look up from their food, as if expecting to encounter 'American Royalty!'

Hopefully, they are not too disappointed, although it is always hard not to feel like a princess, dining in such a beautiful Château! An enormous medieval fireplace, which in winter burns logs the size of tree trunks, dominates the space and stone walls draw one's eye upwards to the amazing vaulted ceiling.

163

Not too large to lose its cosy 'ambiance', the room, with its alcoves and stone pillars, provides the diner with an intimate experience, lit by huge medieval chandeliers and a candle on every table.

Settling back into our chairs, Ronnie orders us each a glass of champagne, as we relax and peruse the menu. Pascal's chef and partner, Philippe has a passion for using local and seasonal produce, which he cooks to the very highest standard of French cuisine and the descriptions of each dish tantalise the taste buds, making the decision a serious business!

For starters, one can choose amongst other delights, a plate of oysters, served with a simple wine vinaigrette and wedges of lemon, pan-fried foie gras or scallops wrapped in pancetta. Similarly varied, the main course, depending on season, may be duck breast served with a delicious red berry jus accompanied by dauphinoise potatoes, or a rich Beef Bourguignon cooked for hours, until the meat just melts in the mouth. The cheese course is a magical mystery tour of local producers' best cheeses, served with grapes and fruit preserves. Finally the desserts, tempt the palette one last time, with a choice of hot chocolate fondant, walnut gâteaux and, of course, every bodies favourite, a Crème Brûlee to die for!

Leaning over to Dad, I help him with the translation and enjoy guiding him through 'la Carte.' Eventually, we all manage to make a decision, just as Pascal arrives to take our order and proffer some delightful 'amuse bouches,' with which to whet out appetite.

Now, as I alluded to earlier, Pascal is a charmer and although, as you might have guessed, he has little or no romantic interest in the ladies, he somehow knows just exactly what to say, to render them putty in his hands! I should not have been surprised, therefore, when he bends down beside me and whispers close to my ear, " Qu'est-ce que vous avez comme secret, Madame?"

Slightly taken aback by this sudden burst of French, clearly aimed at myself, I immediately try to translate in my head, but manage to mishear the pronunciation of the word 'secret', thinking he said 'sucre' meaning sugar and am just about to refuse his kind offer of the same, when Ron steps in to inform me he asked what is my secret? Well, by now, we are all confused, until Pascal coming to our rescue, goes on to whisper, "How do you stay so young, Madame, what is your secret?"

Candlelight and compliments prove irresistible and, gay or not, I dutifully melt like putty in his hands. His task complete, he returns to the kitchen, having guaranteed yet another happy customer!

Leaving the Château later in the evening, Pascal wishes us all 'Bonne Nuit!' and, with the sound of glasses still clinking to toasts of 'Santé!' and the taste of fine cuisine lingering on our palates, we link arms and make our way back across the drawbridge to the waiting car.

Stopping to look over the wall before we head home, our gaze is drawn upwards, to the night sky above. Never before have I seen so many stars and, looking back at the floodlit Château, I put my arm around Dad, so happy he is here to share in our new life.

Chapter Twenty-Three

Open for Business - A Dream Come True!

Sitting in the study towards the end of August, Dad has returned to Ireland and Monsieur Gabin has left the presbytery, with its beautiful new shutters, as immaculate as he himself. All is quiet; the sound of Johnny Halliday no longer drifts from the barn and Ron and I turn our thoughts, once again, to the idea of running our own 'Chambre d'Hôte.'

Tapping into my creative side, I busy myself in the study, attempting to assemble a simple brochure, to promote our new venture and, having downloaded a really lovely picture of the presbytery, with its pale green shutters to adorn the front cover, I carefully type in the words, " L'Ancien Presbytére" at the top and underneath, "Chambre d'Hôte."

Standing back, I think to myself, "Not bad for an amateur!" and, taking the bull by the horns, proceed to embark on what turns out to be a mammoth process of trial and error, interspersed liberally with some rather unfortunate language, which, in my experience, would appear to be an almost inevitable consequence of any project involving a computer. Finally, I come up with a layout that works, showing the blue toile bedroom, with its new en-suite bathroom and the breakfast room, set temptingly with a 'Petit déjeuner' fit for Louis the Fourteenth!

Rather pleased with myself, I run out to the garden to where Ron is busy weeding the borders and proudly present the fruits of my labours. Checking through it, he seems visibly impressed and laughingly agrees he would be tempted to book in for a few nights himself! So, with proof reading complete and the go-ahead from my 'business partner', I disappear up the steps to the computer again, where I eagerly print out twenty more copies, still not quite sure what to do next.

On the kitchen table, steam rises from two cups of strong coffee and, through the open window the sound of bird song, is momentarily interrupted by the buzz of a disorientated bee, as it loses its bearings and pays an uninvited visit to our first board meeting. Gently pointing out the error of its ways, with a quick flick of the tea towel, I launch it kindly in the direction of the window box, where some large red geraniums await its attention.

"Well, if we're really serious about this, Heather, I think it's time we looked at our next move. Where do we go from here?" Silence descends on proceedings and, taking another sip of coffee I suggest, "What about calling in at our local tourist office in Petit Villefranche? It would be useful to talk to someone and I'm sure they could point us in the right direction?" We both agree the little tourist office, tucked away in a cobbled street below the Château, would appear to be a good place to start and, in decisive mode, a joint motion is passed to pay the establishment a visit this afternoon, bringing with us several copies of our new brochure, to give them an idea of what we have to offer.

Bumping along the cobbles in sleepy Petit Villefranche, we manage to get parked just opposite the tourist office. Outside, two rotating stands, filled with brochures on one side and postcards on the other, provide an enticing splash of colour, no doubt placed strategically to catch the attention of passing tourists. Peering past these into the darkness of the interior, I can just make out the figure of a man behind the counter. The office is empty and, judging by his expression, it has been some time since he has been called upon to extol the virtues of the region, or give directions to a group of lost tourists.

Entering the 'Office du Tourisme', we pass the shelves heavy with coloured brochures and gifts from the region and approach the counter. "Bonjour, Monsieur! Vous pouvez nous aider, s'il vous plaît?" Eager to help and, no doubt, relieved to find there is still life on the planet, the man behind the counter introduces himself as Fabrice Desage and, quick to detect, we are not originally from these parts, enquires whence we have come?

A lovely conversation ensues, as we share our story with him and he too goes on to explain he spent several years living and studying in England. An interesting man, Fabrice is almost fluent in English, which proves really helpful, as we go on to explain our desire to open the presbytery as a 'Chambre d'Hôte.'

It turns out he is encouraged to hear of our plans, as the area has a great deal of self-catering accommodation to offer, but very few people providing B&B facilities. Particularly, as he goes on to explain, the 'Horse Trials' commence in just two weeks' time, here in Petit Villefranche, when there is always a great demand for overnight or short-term accommodation.

Happy to hear his enthusiasm, I decide the moment is right to introduce my brochures and, placing them on the counter, I ask Fabrice for his opinion. Carefully reading through the description of what we have to offer, he seems really impressed and kindly remarks, we have a beautiful home, to which he would be very proud to direct any of his customers. In fact, he goes on to suggest, with the Horse Trials imminent, could he possibly have some brochures to put on the counter and would we mind if he were to direct some business our way, over the busy weeks ahead?

Slightly taken aback, at the speed to which we find ourselves propelled into our new business venture, Ronnie asks if there is not something official we should be considering, before going ahead? Fabrice goes on to explain he will give us a pamphlet detailing how to get registered and a list of guidelines regarding required standards to be adhered to, but as we would simply be offering guest accommodation to a small number of people and earning well below the tax threshold, that it would be fine to get started and set everything in motion, as we get up and running.

Leaving the shop, I look back to wave to Fabrice, only to see him carefully place our brochures in a stand on the counter and gently move them towards the front!

The hot afternoon sun beats down on the car, as we climb back in, both rather stunned that we could indeed find ourselves entertaining our first guests, sooner than we thought, but excited too, that after all the renovation work over the last months, we have finally reached this point. Our lives have totally changed and one challenge after another has kept us firmly on our toes, giving us back a purpose in life and slowly building a future for ourselves here in the sun. Looking at each other now, we laugh with a kind of disbelief and silently agree, as we embark on our next venture, bring it on!

Over the next week, we start to plan ahead and take a trip to Angoulême, where we purchase new towels and a handsome breakfast set, with which to adorn the table in our 'Salle à manger.' As per usual, no trip to Angoulême would be complete, without paying a visit to our favourite coffee shop and pâtisserie.

Situated in one of the narrow, cobbled streets off the main square, it is here you find us looking through the vast shop window, at shelves bedecked with sweet temptations of every kind, from huge colourful meringues, to every type of chocolate creation one can conjure up and, believe me, that is quite some feat, as I have a vast imagination when it comes to chocolate!

Peering through the glass, I smile to myself, as I remember the French phrase, 'Lèche Vitrine', meaning to window-shop; unbelievably it literally translates as 'to lick the shop window!' I find myself thinking, how appropriate, and hastily proceed inside, before I am tempted to have a go!

On entering the establishment, we make our way past various stands, piled high with gift boxes, filled with chocolates, cakes and various types of confectionery, towards the long counter or 'comptoir', where we are finally invited to make our choice. Twinkling lights, trained on the delicacies on display, emphasize every aspect of their deliciousness and only serve to make choosing an impossible task, but eventually, as per usual, I plump for a tempting chocolate creation and Ron gives in to the lure of an over-sized meringue!

Round about this time a certain amount of separation anxiety occurs, as we are temporarily parted from our chosen delicacies and directed up stairs to the 'salon du thé', where a pretty, young waitress shows us to our table. "Comme boisson, Madame? Avez-vous choisi?" Looking down the list of delicious hot beverages, I settle upon a hot chocolate and order an espresso for Ronnie, who predictably always goes for the same thing.

Looking round the salon as we relax and settle in, it is clear we are indeed in the city now. At every table, slim, chic French women with impeccable taste sip their espressos delicately and, either pretend to nibble the edge of a pâtisserie or simply refuse to give in to temptation at all. Silently, I decide to eat only half my chocolate creation, as the waitress returns with our order.

Ten minutes later, leaning back in our chairs we both agree everything was absolutely delicious. On the table in front of me, my empty plate reveals my complete lack of willpower and heading back to the car through the busy streets, I vow to myself, as I always do, "On my next visit, I will just have a coffee!"

Back home the halcyon days of late summer stretch on, while upstairs in the presbytery, the blue bedroom sits ready for our first guests. In the en-suite, the glass shower cubicle reflects the morning sunshine, slanting through the open window and, next-door in the bedroom, the double bed awaits resplendent in blue toile. Tea and coffee making facilities rest patiently on the little side table and the small television in the corner has been set up for satellite viewing. Finally, on the marble fireplace, I place my carefully typed notice, "Pas de fumer, s'il vous plait!" and, closing the door behind me, feel content; everything is as I would hope to find it.

Heading down the stairs, past the beautiful Louis the Fourteenth side table on the landing, I delicately re-arrange the brochures depicting things not to be missed in the region, before returning to the kitchen to prepare lunch.

In the garden the next day, while throwing the ball for Murphy, the long awaited phone call finally arrives and running up the steps, I reach the phone just in time, before the answering machine kicks in. Out of breath from my exertions, I manage to get the words out, "Allô, l'Ancien Presbytère."

Of course, I am taken aback, even though we have been preparing for such an eventuality for weeks now and cannot believe when a strange French voice enquires, "Est-ce que c'est L'Ancien Presbytère, Chambre d'Hôte? Je voudrais réserver deux chambres, s'il vous plait!" Thinking on my feet, I try to sound as matter of fact as possible and, in my best French telephone voice declare, rather cowardly I have to admit, "Un moment, Monsieur! Je vous passe à mon mari." and setting the receiver down, I disappear upstairs in search of my French-speaking husband.

The French-speaking husband is not amused, however, as he has been grooming me to take phone calls myself for weeks now, but realising the importance of this call, lifts the phone in our bedroom and does his best to assume the identity of an efficient 'Chambre d'Hôte Propriétaire!'

Replacing the receiver some five minutes later, he has clearly forgotten his irritation over my incompetent telephone skills and beams from ear to ear, declaring 'The Old Presbytery' to be 'open for business'! The booking has been made under the name of a Monsieur Phillipe Meynard and is for three nights. The first night, he will require a double room for his partner, Claudette Buil and himself and the second and third nights, Claudette's parents, also requiring a double room, will join them. The whole family are here to attend the Horse Trials, where Phillipe and Claudette are competitors.

Eagerly, we go back over the arrangements together and agree that Monsieur Meynard and his partner will share the blue bedroom and, as we had discussed previously, if circumstances required it, Ronnie and I will vacate our own bedroom, which is a large double with washing facilities, next door to the 'Grand Salle des Bains.' Giving up our bedroom, we both agree, will be a small price to pay, for what is a great booking, hopefully getting our venture off to a flying start.

Later that evening, as we relax together around the television, Murphy sleeps peacefully at our feet, while we spend some time speculating on the adventure to come. It's as I bend down to ruffle our furry friend's shaggy head, that I suddenly remember his amazing talent as a guard dog and hastily cross my fingers, hoping he will actually afford our first guests a welcome and not 'hound' them off the premises!

Chapter Twenty-Four

A French Affair, Oh La La!

Through the dreamy haze of early morning slumber, somewhere in the distance the sound of the Angelus bell, rings out the call to prayer, as it has done for hundreds of years and, turning over in my cosy bed, I snuggle up to Ron, knowing by now, this means another hour before its time to get up. The darkness, afforded by the heavy shutters, blocks out any memory of what the day ahead has in store; only the narrow shaft of light around the closed and shuttered window whispers the promise of a good day to come.

It's an hour later, with the shrill sound of the alarm clock still ringing in my ears, that the importance of the day finally begins to dawn on me and, sitting up, I find myself staring wide-eyed into the darkness. The realisation I am waking, not in the renovation project, which has occupied my every minute for the last ten months, but in 'The Old Presbytery, Chambre d'Hôte,' sets me to thinking, "not a million miles from here, our first guests will be packing and heading this way!"

The thought is quick to put any idea of further slumber well and truly out of my head, as I realise I have a matter of hours to turn my comfy bedroom into a luxury double for Claudette Buil's parents, arriving the next day. Eager to have everything just right for our first guests, my aim is to have the two rooms ready for inspection and, Ron and I, like a couple of professionals, prepared in plenty of time to deliver a warm welcome.

Together, we both leap out of bed and take it in turns to throw open the shutters around the house, allowing the bright morning sunshine to flood in, filling us and the house with enthusiasm for our new venture and convincing me of the joy I shall have, sharing this beautiful place with our guests.

Later in the morning I return to my bedroom, laden down with crisp new bedding and fluffy towels. Carefully I wash the little sink by the window, until it shines like fine bone china and placing two hand-towels on the adjacent rail, I strip the bed and make it up again, with new sheets. Finally, setting the two remaining chunky bath towels invitingly at the bottom of the bed, all that's left is to check the tea and coffee making facilities and place the obligatory 'Pas de fumer' sign on the marble fireplace. Stepping back, I catch my breath and declare the job done!

Sharing lunch together on the terrace, later in the morning, we compare notes and agree the house is ready to go. Bedrooms sit resplendent in anticipation of their new occupants, all bathrooms have received their final polish and, in the dining room, the table is set for breakfast, where the new coffee machine is primed and ready to percolate.

We linger over a particularly tasty slice of 'Tarte Tatin' and allow ourselves to relax, in the knowledge that a phone call from Monsieur Meynard last night confirmed their arrival time to be seven o'clock in the evening. Still another six hours away, I think to myself, plenty of time before we have to take on the mantle of the perfect hosts.

Ron, having cut the grass yesterday suggests, as his jobs are complete, he might drive over to Agens and return the enormous petrol strimmer, James had lent him earlier in the week. "I could take Murphy for the ride and give him a bit of exercise, in the hope he'll be asleep in his basket by the time the guests arrive. I should only be an hour or two."

Peace descends on the presbytery. The village is enjoying siesta time and with Ron and Murphy safely off the premises, I stretch out on a sun bed in a shady corner of the garden and have a quick after-noon nap. Eventually, the thought of lunch dishes on

174

the kitchen shelf draws me back up the steps. I close the door to the garden behind me, glad to feel the cool interior of the house, after the heat outside and return to the kitchen and the job in hand.

It's as I place the last dish in the dishwasher and do the final wipe of the shelves, that the shrill ring of the telephone disturbs the silence of my tranquil afternoon and sends me scurrying from the kitchen to where it rests on the bureau, just below our picture of the deep pink peonies.

"Allô, L'Ancien Presbytère!" I trot out my usual greeting, expecting to hear Katie or Richard, my Sister or perhaps even Dad, but lulled into a false sense of security, I do not expect the dulcet tones of Monsieur Meynard, especially after his phone call last night to inform us of his seven o'clock arrival!

Gathering all my faculties and, concentrating really hard, I hear him explain, the lovely weather has urged them to set out early and he hopes it won't be inconvenient, but they have just arrived in Saint-Allier and are parked opposite the Boulangerie awaiting directions.

Well, by now, my heart is just about to jump out of my rather too casual T-shirt; this is not how things are supposed to happen! Where is Ron with his perfect French when you need him? But there is no time to panic and manfully taking on the role of la propriètaire, I suggest in my best French accent, that he is actually just next to the 'Presbytery' and find myself volunteering to come out and direct him to the back entrance.

Unfortunately, despite my previous plan not to panic, I drop the phone on the bureau, where it rests below the peonies and make for the front door. The bright sunlight hits me as I step out into the street and, making my way around to the right of the building, I find Monsieur Meynard and his partner Claudette, parked at the side of the road in a rather sleek maroon convertible.

Approaching the open window, I bend down to greet them. " Bonjour, Monsieur Meynard et Mademoiselle Buil!   Je suis

Madame Kennedy, la propriètaire de L'Ancien Presbytère. Suivez moi, s'il vous plait!" Hoping they've got the gist, I set off pointing them in the direction of the lane.

Alas, as I arrive at the front door of the house, a draft of air from the open windows inside catches the door, which Monsieur Fournier has ensured is in perfect working order and it dutifully closes with a solid bang! My brain registers the problem immediately and quickly I search my pockets, to no avail, for the key, which, of course, still rests firmly on the other side of the now locked front door!

"Don't panic!" I think to myself yet again. The back door is sure to be open and any thought of being locked out is firmly put to the back of my mind, as I attempt to gather my composure and lead my guests down the lane, through the grand gates of the presbytery, to where they can park safely at the foot of the steps.

It is at this point, as my guests disembark from the car, that I get my first chance to greet them close up. Monsieur Meynard, a tall attractive man in his mid forties, has thick dark hair sleeked back impeccably; he is wearing a colourful check shirt, tucked neatly over slim hips, into a tight fitting pair of jodhpurs. He steps forward with confidence and introduces Claudette, a petite young woman in her late twenties, with matching jodhpurs and unruly blonde curls. She looks up admiringly at him, as he explains they have stabled their horses nearby and are keen to get in and freshen up.

"Bien sûr, Monsieur! C'est pas de problème!" I gush enthusiastically, as I run up the steps, genuinely believing the door, which is rarely locked, will open and allow me to turn around and welcome my guests, in the carefully planned manner, Ron and I have rehearsed so many times over the last week.

Arriving at the top, I place my hand on the door handle and push. Like a bad dream, the door won't budge and a flash back to earlier reminds me, because I was alone in the house, unusually I had turned the key in the lock, when I came in from the garden. Suddenly, everything moves in slow motion and turning to my guests, I desperately search my French vocabulary for the words, "I am locked out!"

At the bottom of the steps, my two clients look confused, no doubt having never come across this particular problem in the past on arriving at a Chambres d'Hôtes, for which they had prior booking. Thinking on my feet, I apologise profusely and suggest they might like to drive into Petit Villefranche, just five minutes down the road, where they could enjoy a coffee, until my husband returns in about half an hour with his key.

Smugly, I pat myself on the back, having come up with an excellent plan, which will remove the problem until Ronnie's return. Alas, Phillipe Meynard has other ideas and, not wishing to be put off, he points to the open kitchen window and asks for a ladder. Truthfully, I reply that I haven't got one to hand, but unwilling to accept defeat, he casts his eye around the garden and it comes to rest on the small white ladder, resting innocently against the 'blue blot' at the bottom of the garden.

The next minute, I find myself standing beside Claudette, watching in amazement, as Phillipe sprints down the garden and returns with the 'blue blot' ladder, which he carefully places up against the wall below the kitchen window and embarks on a perilously, wobbly climb, to the sill above. Reaching the top, like a man possessed, he launches himself, James Bond style, through the open window and disappears head first into the kitchen beyond, his black riding boots the last thing we see, as all goes suddenly quiet. Inside I think to myself, thank goodness Murphy isn't here, or I dread to think the reception he would have received!

Several seconds pass, until suddenly Phillipe's head pops up in the window, his immaculate black hair standing uncharacteristically on end but with a triumphant grin from ear to ear. Heading out to the hall, he opens the door and bizarrely performs my well-rehearsed welcome speech, as he invites me into my own Chambre d'Hôte!

It may not seem possible, but at this point I manage to gather myself together and, helping them up the steps with their bags, I amazingly resume my composure. Quickly I revert to my role as propriètaire, trying desperately to pretend the last twenty minutes never happened!

Inside, the presbytery sits resplendent in it's tranquillity and, requesting them to "Suivez-moi!" I lead the way up the stairs to the blue toile bedroom, where, in an effort to look professional, I demonstrate the facilities on offer in their room, with which they seem very happy. Obviously relieved, however, at having breached my defences and finally gaining entry, I can tell they just want to put their bags down and settle in; so wishing them 'Bonnes Vacances!', I hand Monsieur Meynard his room key and disappear down the stairs, to the relative safety of the 'rez-de-chaussée!'

Fifteen minutes later, Ronnie arrives at the back gate and, entering the garden, parks the car by the barn. Climbing the steps, closely followed by Murphy, he joins me in the kitchen. "Whose is the car in the drive?", he asks innocently. Slowly, I recount the unexpected early arrival of our guests and the series of events which followed.

Ron sympathises, but as the story unfolds, he finds it hard not to see the funny side and, putting his arm around me laughs, saying, "Never mind, dear, at least you won't forget the arrival of our first guests in a hurry! By the way, have they everything they need in the room?"

"Everything except a bottle of water, which I meant to leave on the tray." I reply. " But they're bound to be thirsty after their journey, Heather. Why don't you pop up with it, so they can put the kettle on?" "I thought I might hand it to them later, when they come down." I reply rather sheepishly. " But that would be too late. There's no use providing tea and coffee making facilities, if you don't supply fresh water. Here you are; it'll only take a few seconds. Leave it up to their room."

Against my better judgement, but keen to provide an excellent service, I take the large bottle of water and head up the stairs to the blue toile bedroom, where I respectfully knock on the door. Silence follows. I knock again. Perhaps they didn't hear me? Nothing. Then I notice the door isn't quite closed and, remembering having passed Monsieur Meynard his room key, I make the unfortunate decision, that as the door isn't locked, I should put my head around and hand deliver my gift of water. Big mistake!

There on my beautiful blue toile bed is Monsieur Meynard, wearing nothing but a smile and from under the duvet, Claudette's two eyes peep over the top, reflecting the look of horror in my own! "Pardonez-moi!", I blurt out, as I set the water down and escape post haste down the stairs.

At the bottom, Ronnie looks at me quizzically, but pushing past him I run out the door and don't stop running until I reach the farthest corner of the garden, where I bury my face in my hands, unable to believe what I have just done. Ron finally arrives, still puffing and panting and gasps, "What happened?" It's several seconds before I can whisper through my fingers, "I've just seen Monsieur Meynard naked on the blue toile bed!"

Hidden in the corner of the garden, surrounded by nothing but birdsong, we look at each other in disbelief, before bursting into hysterical laughter. What an unbelievable start to our new venture! "Well, at least that explains Phillipe's determination to breach our defences!", declares Ron, setting us both off again!

A few hours later, as Phillipe and Claudette head out for something to eat, they pass me in the hallway and, stopping to ask for recommendation of a local eatery, make no reference to the 'French Farce,' in which they unwittingly found themselves the central characters. On the contrary, they seem very happy, as they wish us a 'Bonne Soirée' and skip down the steps to their awaiting car.

Over the next two days, despite a rather unconventional start, 'The Old Presbytery Chambre d'Hôte' comes into its own. Our guests are greeted in the morning with the smell of freshly percolated coffee, as it wafts its way up the winding staircase and our breakfast table is laden with freshly baked croissants, pains au raisin and pains au chocolat, still warm from the boulangerie.

Claudette's parents arrive the next day, at the stated time and Ron and I finally get the chance to deliver our well-rehearsed welcome speech. They turn out to be a lovely family and are a joy to have around the house, as they come and go, back and forth to the horse trials in Petit Villefranche.

On their last night, we are delighted to discover they have managed to secure a booking at the Château for their evening meal and, before they set off, we share in the good news of Claudette's success in the afternoon's jumping event.

The morning of their departure arrives all too soon, as Ron and I are just getting into the swing of things. Standing around the bureau in the hall, in the shadow of the pink peonies, Monsieur Meynard writes us a cheque to cover both bookings, while Claudette's Mother very kindly remarks on the comfort of their room and compliments me on the restoration and decoration of the presbytery. Meanwhile, in the background, I notice Claudette making the first entry in our new 'Guest Book!'

Finally, as they pick up their bags ready to leave, Ron reaches out his hand to Monsieur Meynard and, in French, says how nice it was to have met them all, while apologising discretely for any inconvenience at the start of their stay. With a mischievous twinkle in his eye, Monsieur Meynard surprises us all by replying in perfect English, "Oh, don't worry about that. It was all very amusing!"

Standing at the top of the steps, we wave our first guests off the premises on their homeward journey and, as they disappear into the lane beyond, Ron and I breathe a sigh of relief. We have survived our first venture into the hospitality business. It might have started off like an episode of 'Fawlty Towers,' but when we read our first entry in the new 'Guest Book,' our hearts are lifted, as Claudette describes the presbytery as the perfect place to stay and Ronnie and I, as the perfect hosts!

Chapter Twenty-Five

Saying, "Merci," with a Beef Bourguignon

Over the next days, Fabrice Desage at the tourist office continues to send us a steady trickle of guests, while we apply for registration and await our first inspection. 'The Old Presbytery,' I am delighted to report, is beginning to run like a well-oiled machine and, needless to say we haven't caught any more of our guests 'in the all together,' with each one now enjoying a warm welcome, through the front door, in the conventional manner! The story of our first venture into the hospitality business has, however, proven a great tale to dine out on and never fails to enliven even the dullest of dinner parties!

With a bit of time between guests this week, you find me busily preparing a meal for Chantal, Henri and little Amèlie. This is something I have been intending to do for some time now, in order to thank them for their help over the summer and the many times, when they have invited us to join them round their table.

Following a Delia Smith recipe, I've been in the kitchen since early morning and have finally managed to produce a 'Beef Bourguignon,' which I can leave to simmer gently on the hob, until our guests arrive at around seven. Carefully getting as much flavour into the old French classic as I could, I sautéed shallots and garlic, with bacon lardons and fresh woodland mushrooms. Browning great chunks of Charolais beef and throwing in a 'bouquet garni' and a couple of bay leaves, before finally dousing the whole thing in a delicious bottle of Burgundy.

In the late afternoon sunshine, with a tasty aroma from the kitchen wafting through the air, we busy ourselves setting a table for supper in the garden. The presbytery looks resplendent with its majestic stone steps but therein lies it's 'Achilles' Heel' in respect of dining al fresco. By this I refer to the number of times one has to run up and down the aforementioned structure, in order to set the table and serve the food!

A future plan will be to create a summer kitchen in the cellar, to the left of the steps. The door there leads directly onto the terrace and behind it a room with beautiful stone walls and a massive beamed ceiling, which would lend itself perfectly to the job. Although the floor at the moment is just beaten earth, if tiled with cool terracotta tiles and fitted with a simple sink, some cupboards, a fridge and a cooker, it would be perfect for entertaining.

There are so many projects still left to be tackled at the presbytery; it will keep us busy for years to come, but, for the moment the main house has eaten up all our savings and, therefore, plans for converting the barn into two self catering gîtes, along with the summer kitchen, will have to be put on hold for the present. Our idea is to save the proceeds from the 'Chambre d'Hôte' business in a separate account, with the aim of eventually starting work on these projects, as soon as funds allow.

In the meantime back in the present, the summer kitchen remains but a dream and, as the church bell chimes seven times, the sound of Amèlie's laughter announces the imminent arrival of our guests. Placing a bottle of Pineau, some Ricard for Henri and juice for Amèlie on the table, we greet our neighbours with the three kisses, before, relaxed and happy in each other's company, we enjoy an 'apéro' together, in the late summer heat of what is turning out to be a beautiful, balmy evening.

Around us, dusk begins to fall and, pausing from our conversation, we watch the bats, as they leave the barn for the night. Handing out starters of fresh smoked salmon, tossed salad and wedges of lemon, out of the corner of my eye, I notice Ronnie chasing Amèlie round the big walnut tree, pretending to be 'une chauve-souris', or in English 'a bat' and, looking up at my happy carefree husband, I call them to return to the table, where "Le repas est prêt à manger."

The starter having gone down well, served with a light crisp Chablis, I find time at last to sit back and relax. Looking over at Henri, I notice he has made an effort this evening and is wearing a pair of cool cotton trousers and, having abandoned the sleeveless vest, has replaced it with a loose fitting short-sleeved shirt.

We chat happily about village affairs and particularly Saint-Allier Sud, our little corner of the village, where Henri informs me the Parisiens have returned to their home in the outskirts of Paris and Inès, Jacques' widow, has put her house up for sale, as she plans to move back to Angoulême, to be near her parents.

A lull in the conversation allows me to gather up the dishes and head back up the steps to the kitchen, where the 'Beef Bourguignon' still simmers gently on the hob. Quickly, I blanche some green beans and lightly pan fry them with a little garlic, before emptying them into a hot serving dish. Returning back down the steps with the beans in one hand and a huge basket of fresh crusty bread in the other, I mentally make a note to move the summer kitchen project to the top of the 'to do' list!

Descending finally with the 'pièce de résistance', my Beef Bourguignon, I place it at the centre of the table. Its rich dark colour contrasts beautifully with the bright green interior of the huge ceramic bowl it's served in, while the aromas of tender beef and burgundy wine fill the night air. Henri and Chantal look impressed and I breathe a sigh of relief; their praise means a lot to me. Being French, I know how highly they rate the culinary arts.

Well, thanks to Delia and some impressive ingredients, my 'Bourguignon' passes the test with flying colours! Henri and Chantal, pleasantly surprised, sing its praises, as they enthusiastically mop up the rich dark sauce with chunks of crusty bread.

By the time dessert is served, darkness has well and truly fallen and only two lamps on the wall of the presbytery and the moonlight above illuminate our little gathering, at the foot of the steps. Meanwhile, flickering candles in the centre of the table reflect the laughter and love shared between us, as crickets create the sound track to this perfect evening, only interrupted by the clink of glasses.

With dessert, conversation moves on to the subject of marriage. Hardly surprising, as Chantal and Henri are still relative newly weds, having tied the knot only a few years earlier. They are keen to recount their perfect day and both vie eagerly to fill us in on every aspect. Chantal describes her dress in minute detail and explains how she had opted out of the traditional veil, in favour of a white silk top hat, wrapped around with a broad ribbon and tied at the back with a large bow.

Henri, on the other hand, can't wait to fill us in, on the old wedding customs, still performed in their tiny village, of which he and Chantal were eager participants. Apparently, after the church ceremony, the bride and groom return to their village, where the groom selects a tree of his choice. The wedding party then stand around in a circle, cheering him on loudly, as still dressed in his wedding attire, it is his job to chop the tree down for his new bride.

Judging by Henri's gestures and the twinkle in his eye, at this point of the story, it becomes obvious that the size of the chosen tree is designed to reflect, in no small way, on the virility of the groom! Henri, ever eager to impress his young bride, had, of course, been rather optimistic in his choice of tree, resulting in him working up quite a sweat, before everyone jumped back cheering, as the tree fell at Chantal's feet.

A relieved groom, now aided by the whole wedding party, loaded the tree onto the back of a trailer, bedecked in white ribbons and flowers and pulled along by a local farmer on his tractor. Finally, as daintily as possible, it was Chantal's job to be helped onto the trailer, where sitting astride the tree, she is paraded triumphantly through the streets of the village, to loud cheers and clapping. Eventually, arriving at the 'salle des fêtes,' in time for the wedding reception, where, like all French fêtes, everyone partied well into the early hours!

Ron and I, fascinated by their story, are left with a lasting image in our minds, of Chantal in her lovely dress and top hat, sat astride the tree and, as Ron tops up our glasses with some sweet dessert wine, we all fall about laughing again, as Henri boasts unashamedly of the size of his sapling!

Eventually, Amèlie is beginning to yawn and we all agree it is time to say goodnight. Ronnie and I walk our neighbours down to the gate, where we share our three kisses again and wish each other 'Bonne nuit!' Making our way back up the garden to clear the table, I reflect back to my life in Belfast, where we lived in the same street for many years and never knew our neighbours. Now wrapped in the warmth of the still evening air, I am so grateful to be part of this community, that has taken Ronnie and I to their hearts without question and made us one of their own.

Chapter Twenty-Six

Santé! to 'The Old Presbytery' and our New Life in the Sun

The following day we take things easy and, around four in the afternoon, after a bit of light gardening, jump in the blue blot to cool down. Floating on my back, I stare up at the sky with its wispy white clouds and listen to the sound of the water gently lapping against the side of the pool, until Ron, balancing precariously at the top of the wobbly, white ladder, jumps in beside me. Together we enjoy a refreshing dip, before climbing out and wrapping ourselves in towels, we head back to the presbytery to dry off.

Just as I get to the top of the steps, hair dripping water onto the wooden floorboards and bare feet leaving damp footprints up the hall, I am stopped in my tracks by the sound of the front door bell. Still holding my brightly coloured towel in place, I tentatively open the door, just wide enough to pop my head around.

"Bonjour, Madame! On cherche deux chambres, pour quatre personnes s'il vous plait? Est-ce que vous avez des chambres libre?" In front of me in the street outside, a lovely young couple and their two small children look up hopefully. The gentleman goes on to explain, they have just driven all the way from Paris and, after calling at the tourist office, Monsieur Desage, had given them our brochure.

Apologising for my rather soggy appearance, I happily reply, "Bien sûr!" and ask them to drive down the lane to the back entrance, where they can park their car. Post-haste I roughly dry off and, while Ron runs upstairs to get changed, I grab my shorts and t-shirt from the chair in the living room and pull them on, just in time to welcome them at the top of the steps.

Luckily, I keep the two guest rooms ready at all times for such eventualities and with a great feeling of satisfaction, I guide the tired little band of dusty travellers up the stairs to the blue toile bedroom, where Monsieur et Madame Debray look delighted to be able to set down their bags at last.

Across the hall, together we install the children in the twin bedroom, at the front of the house, its freshly decorated walls in cream and duck egg blue are soft and welcoming and the children, quick to jump on the beds and make themselves at home, chatter happily to their Mum in French, as I excuse myself to finish drying my hair and allow the family time to settle in.

About fifteen minutes later, Ron and I are dressed and just pouring a glass of wine, before starting the dinner, when Madame Debray pops her head around the kitchen door and enquires politely, "After their long hot journey, could they possibly take the children for a dip in the pool?"

"Of course," I reply, glad they feel so relaxed in our home and, checking they have enough towels, I close the kitchen door over, just in time to hear the excited shrieks of the children, as they skip down the steps in the direction of the pool.

Standing in the kitchen with its blue and white tiles, we look down the garden, to where our latest guests splash happily in the 'blue blot,' after their long hot journey from Paris. The shrieks of joy from the children, as they splash about in the cooling water, filter back to my ears and echo the feeling of joy I have inside. A few years earlier, it seemed we had lost everything and this beautiful place has given us a second chance. Tearing our eyes away from the happy scene, Ronnie pulls me towards him and lifting our glasses simultaneously, we drink a toast to 'The Old Presbytery' and our new life in the sun.

188